"This book will challenge you to rethink [...] ers who seriously question our faith, and it [...] to point them toward the only One who ca[...] hope."

Kevin Ezell, President, North American Mission Board, Southern Baptist Convention

"To be alive today is to be at the intersection of worldviews. Different worldviews compete for allegiance, but Dan DeWitt clearly demonstrates that there are really only two worldviews in constant conflict: theism versus nihilism. The superiority of the Christian worldview is demonstrated not only by its inherent truth claims, but also by the tragic inadequacy of nihilism. DeWitt sets the issue clearly in his title: it's *Jesus or Nothing*. Any thinking person will benefit from reading this important new book."

R. Albert Mohler Jr., President and Joseph Emerson Brown Professor of Christian Theology, The Southern Baptist Theological Seminary

"Life really does boil down to Jesus or nothing. Without Christ, we are left with relative morals, meaningless lives, and no hope. Dan is a learned theologian, but never arrogant or judgmental. He has a genuine compassion for those in search of truth, no matter how big or 'dangerous' their questions are. *Jesus or Nothing* is a book that matters, because its proposition is the ultimate matter."

Josh Wilson, award-winning singer/songwriter

"DeWitt courageously takes us to life's great intersection. There we find the atheist's theory of nothing and the Christian theory of everything. Decision and destiny hang in the balance for all."

Jack D. Eggar, President/CEO, Awana

"*Jesus or Nothing* is a little book about a big God. If you are a skeptic or a minister to skeptics, you should read this book about the God who is conspicuously there and who aims to reconcile sinners to himself through Christ."

Denny Burk, author, *What Is the Meaning of Sex?*

"The truthfulness of the claims of Scripture matters, and those claims have been—and will continue to be—defended often. But another, more basic question matters as well: What is the value, meaning, and purpose of life without God? Dan DeWitt brilliantly demonstrates that the choice truly is *Jesus or Nothing.*"

Timothy Paul Jones, author, *Misquoting Truth: A Guide to the Fallacies of Bart Ehrman's* Misquoting Jesus

"Dan DeWitt knows his stuff. It is apparent that he's familiar with everyone from Chesterton to Lewis to Schaeffer, not only in the ideas set forth in this book, but in his gentle, good-humored tone as well. In a culture where it can feel like Christianity is on the defensive, Dan reminds us that the gospel is beautiful beyond reason and completely reasonable."

Andrew Peterson, singer/songwriter; author, The Wingfeather Saga series

"Citing everyone from Hawking to Chesterton, Dan shows not only the reasonableness but also the beauty of the gospel of Christ. *Jesus or Nothing* provides a concise and thoughtful resource for engaging secularists and academics in a city like Boston, where I live and minister."

Bland Mason, Pastor, City on a Hill Church, Boston, Massachusetts; baseball chapel leader to the Boston Red Sox

"*Jesus or Nothing* will take you on a journey through the hope of the gospel and cause you to engage those seeking answers to life's most important questions with grace and truth."

Andraé Robinson, Pastor, Cornerstone Church, South
Los Angeles, California

"Dan DeWitt artfully and accurately presents the big picture of one of the most important battles for hearts in our day. Atheism is often portrayed as the only intelligent worldview, but this book dispels the fog of that myth. I heartily recommend *Jesus or Nothing* to anyone struggling to sort through the shrill, confusing voices trying to tell us what matters most."

Ted Cabal, General Editor, *The Apologetics Study Bible*

"*Jesus or Nothing* addresses the question that believers and nonbelievers alike are afraid to ask—'What if I'm wrong?' In an increasingly post-Christian context, Dan contrasts these two worldviews and guides the reader to the exclusive foundation for human flourishing found in the gospel."

Andy Frew, singer/songwriter; Worship Pastor, Crossridge Church, Surrey, British Columbia

"Dan DeWitt paints a beautiful portrait of Jesus with all the strokes of a fine painter. *Jesus or Nothing* shows us how to engage our skeptic friends in the grandeur of a story unique and true. DeWitt's personal enjoyment is etched throughout the painting, exploding with the reality of Jesus and the truth of the gospel. This is a recommended read for all who want to reveal the awesome beauty of Jesus to those who are choosing *Nothing*."

David Clifford, Events Manager, Desiring God

"The ultimate human question has always been that of meaning—the meaning of life, the meaning of death, the meaning of everything. Dan DeWitt reminds us again that meaning is always and necessarily grounded in God, and God is known only through Christ in the gospel. Apart from him, all pleasure, success, and happiness that may (or may not) come your way ultimately adds up to nothing. Biblically solid and culturally aware, DeWitt weaves together references to Pascal, *Toy Story 3*, Richard Dawkins, John Lennon, and Aleksandr Solzhenitsyn to argue that there are only two roads: the gospel or emptiness, Jesus or nothing. Accessible and enjoyable works on apologetics that are also richly thought provoking are a rarity; Dan DeWitt manages the task beautifully. This book will encourage and challenge many."

Grant Horner, Associate Professor of Renaissance and
Reformation, The Master's College; author, *Meaning at the Movies*

JESUS

OR

NOTHING

Dan DeWitt

Foreword by RUSSELL D. MOORE

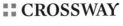

WHEATON, ILLINOIS

Trade paperback ISBN: 978-1-4335-4046-2
PDF ISBN: 978-1-4335-4047-9
Mobipocket ISBN: 978-1-4335-4048-6
ePub ISBN: 978-1-4335-4049-3

Library of Congress Cataloging-in-Publication Data
DeWitt, Dan, 1977–
   Jesus or nothing / Dan DeWitt; foreword by Russell D. Moore.
     pages cm
   Includes bibliographical references.
   ISBN 978-1-4335-4046-2 (tp)
   1. Christianity and atheism. 2. Apologetics. 3. Nothing (Philosophy) 4. Nihilism (Philosophy) 5. Bible. Colossians—Criticism, interpretation, etc. I. Title.
BR128.A8D49   2014
261.2'1—dc23   2013030076

Crossway is a publishing ministry of Good News Publishers.

VP		24	23	22	21	20	19	18	17	16	15	14
15	14	13	12	11	10	9	8	7	6	5	4	3	2	1

To April Joy,
my beautiful and faithful bride

Contents

Foreword

Russell D. Moore

Atheists are easy to hate, until you can't help but love one.

What I mean is that, despite all our supposed seculariization, it takes a certain sort of cultural courage to say, "I don't believe in God." Since that's the case, most of the high-profile people proclaiming as much in public are people with adrenaline firing in a quest to disprove or ridicule faith, especially the Christian faith. But judging atheists by the pamphleteers and the professionally irreligious is akin to unbelievers judging Christians by our most outrageous prosperity-hawking television evangelists.

Most people learn to love atheists by learning to love an atheist—maybe a son or a daughter, or an old college roommate; someone who just can't believe anymore that at the nub of this whirling universe there's a Father. When one knows, and loves, someone like that, one realizes that this isn't part of some conspiratorial plot to attack the faith. This is someone who has lost his or her story—and is looking for a way to make sense of a cosmos filled with quasars and waterfalls, of pythons and parasites.

The book you hold in your hand—or view on your screen—isn't an argument. It's not more intellectual ammunition designed to help you win a debate over coffee. It is something I saw buzzing about in the author's life for years—as he learned to love some atheists. He didn't see them as projects or prizes—some sort of spiritual taxidermy to hang on his mantle if he won them to Christ. He saw them as friends—to be witnessed to, of course, but also to be listened to. This book is meant to awaken your imagination in two directions—first, toward the wonder of what it means that this story we find ourselves in is really true. There really is a dynamically alive ex-corpse who is bending all of history toward himself. You really are accepted, and forgiven, and welcome if you're hidden in him. You really have nothing to fear—from your past guilt or from your future casket. But this book will also turn your imagination toward those around you who just can't find that old, old story to be good, good news.

The author is a bright Christian scholar, a winsome Christian teacher. But he's also one who knows what it is like to follow his Lord toward sitting down with those far from the kingdom—and with a provocative tranquility show them a story that, if as true as we believe it is, upends everything. The kingdom of God is not, the Scriptures tell us, a matter of talk but of power. This book is electric with kingdom power—the kind of power that casts out darkness, tears down strongholds, and tells a story just wild enough to love.

Introduction

The Power of Nothing

He saw Nothing. Beyond the shrubbery in his front yard, he saw Nothing. The landscaping pointed simply to itself and not to a grand designer in the sky. The bushes didn't host fairies or goblins. They had nothing to do with gods or holy books. They just were.

That's how Mark Bauerlein, professor of English at Emory University, describes his teenage conversion to atheism.[1] Mark's experience is not uncommon. Another skeptic once shared with me that he became an atheist as a boy shortly after a close friend died. The thought of his friend peering into his preteen adolescent activities sort of creeped him out. And so he came to grips with Nothing. There was Nothing beyond death. There was no heaven. And there was no God.

Sometimes Nothing can be quite therapeutic. It's likely that Nothing has soothed your fears at some point in your life. Parents calm their children with the words, "There's nothing in the closet." No monsters. No bogeymen. Nothing. You can go back to bed and rest in peace: this Nothing can't hurt you.

This is why the recent atheistic marketing campaign caused such a stir. For many the message connected with a deep longing for ultimate liberation: "God probably doesn't exist. Go ahead and enjoy the rest of your life." This proposal touches a nerve in the believing community as well. Many professing Christians, for all practical purposes, live as functional atheists with little regard for God's sovereign rule over their daily lives.

This is not to say that atheists stop with Nothing. But for many, perhaps most, Nothing is where they begin. That's where it began for Zach. He grew up in a conservative Christian home in the bluegrass state of Kentucky. His devout parents sent him to a fundamentalist Christian school from kindergarten though high school graduation. He was well versed in the sort of things that make Nothing all the more appealing.

After eighteen years of emotional revival services, fiery church business meetings, silly youth group antics, endless rules and regulations, and leadership resignations due to moral downfalls, he was ready for something else. And he found it in the local community college. He breathed deeply the fresh air of intellectual diversity. For the first time in his life he felt truly free.

He first contemplated the possibilities of Nothing in a biology class his second semester, where his professor presented the merits of evolution. The theory was nearly forbidden in his private high school. It was worse than a four-letter word. Yet here it was discussed in a rational and persuasive manner. Now when Zach looked out at the world, with its own natural explanations, he saw Nothing. And it was beautiful.

Zach later transferred to a large state university to pursue a degree in humanities. He spent the summer after his junior year with a group of students from a humanist campus organization serving the poor in Haiti. He caringly handed food rations to impoverished youth amid trash heaps. He and his colleagues toiled beneath the summer sun to make a difference one child at a time. The grateful, yet sunken, brown eyes of starving boys and girls were more than enough to make his sacrifice seem relatively insignificant, yet powerfully satisfying. He didn't do it for religion. He did it for hungry children.

He always thought that if he embraced Nothing, he would instantly morph into some sort of morally reprehensible monster. He quickly discarded this misconception, along with a host of others he had heard throughout childhood. Early in his senior year he made the dreaded phone call to his parents and told them he was no longer a Christian. They were devastated. At the fork in the road between Jesus and Nothing, he chose Nothing.

And who can blame him?

His story is repeated countless times at colleges across America. I've had the wonderful privilege of meeting many students like Zach over the last several years as I've led a campus ministry at a secular school. I've been pleasantly surprised by the healthy discussions that are possible between Christians and skeptics. All too often caricatures of both sides thwart meaningful relationships.

We started our ministry with three seminars, one a month, spread out over an academic semester. Perhaps the titles of our events illustrate why a number of skeptics regularly attended our gatherings: "What I Hate about Religion," "What I've Learned from Atheism," and last but not least, "What I Love about the Gospel." From the beginning we sought common ground to engage in meaningful conversations. Christian ministries regularly limit themselves to monologue—we longed for dialogue.

Though I'm now the dean of a Bible college, I still have regular opportunities to speak to university students. When given the occasion to address the topic of the Christian faith, I often use the book of Colossians to outline my presentation. There are numerous paths a discourse about faith can take, and I've found that the simplicity of Paul's short letter provides helpful parameters for demonstrating the gospel's unique ability to provide an objective basis for human flourishing.

My presentation of the gospel, grounded in Colossians, has evolved over the years. And so have I. My understanding of both the gospel and the human condition continue to deepen and flavor the way I talk about Jesus. In many ways this book is a culmination of the interactions, conversations, relationships, and dialogues about the gospel that I've shared with thoughtful and intelligent students, believers and unbelievers alike.

This is a book for Zach, and many like him who have considered walking away from their childhood faith in favor of a different worldview. I hope to contrast the narrative of the gospel with what I believe to be an inevitable nihilism that permeates a godless universe.

I recognize that my words cannot—in and of themselves—convince a cynic or convert a sinner. Yet, it is my aim, and my prayer, that this short book will encourage believers in their love of the gospel, challenge skeptics in their rejection of it, and assist Christian parents and leaders as they contend for the faith once for all delivered to the saints (Jude 1:3).

My goal is not to offer finely tuned apologetic arguments—though there are several references to such defenses—but instead to ask the reader to envision what the world would look like if the gospel were actually true. If this book achieves anything, I hope it shows, even to some small measure, that Christianity is both plausible and desirable. And who knows: maybe it's also true. Just imagine.

Welcome to the human epic of Jesus or Nothing.

1

The Tale of Two Stories

It was the best of times, it was the worst of times,
it was the age of wisdom, it was the age of foolish-
ness, it was the epoch of belief, it was the epoch
of incredulity, it was the season of Light, it was
the season of Darkness, it was the spring of hope,
it was the winter of despair, we had everything
before us, we had nothing before us . . .

Charles Dickens

Long before Charles Dickens penned *A Tale of Two Cities* depicting the class struggle between the French bourgeois and the aristocracy, Saint Augustine described a more costly battle. His classic work *The City of God* outlined the conflict between seeking fulfillment in the fleeting pleasures of this world (the City of Man) and finding ultimate purpose from above (the City of God). The epic of two cities, the tale of two stories, outlines the history of human existence.

Consider the responses to the terrorist attacks of 2001: churches overflowed in the days following the tragic acts now remembered simply as 9/11. However, beyond the national calls to prayer and the revival of church attendance across America, another movement emerged to capture the attention of book publishers and commentators around the world. The campaign quickly earned the title of The New Atheism and not only challenged religion's answer to the problem of evil, but also directed public attention to religion itself as the source of all evil.

In their 2010 book *The New Atheist Novel: Fiction, Philosophy and Polemic after 9/11* authors Arthur Bradley and Andrew Tate describe the New Atheist movement as an attempt to establish a cultural narrative. As an atheist and a Christian respectively, the authors provide an interesting critique of the new movement: "For us, the New Atheists' desire to create a new mythos might also explain why they are so interested in literature: what starts out as science-as-novel could almost be said to reach its logical conclusion in the novel-as-science."[1]

These two accounts—theism and atheism—mark the polar extremes of humanity's quest for truth. They simplify and summarize the most complex of all theories and philosophies. And they cannot both be true. Thus, humanity stands at an impasse facing the solemn choice between the City of God and the City of Man. The central plot of every narrative is built upon this decision. This is where every story begins.

The Story of Nothing

G. K. Chesterton, the British journalist and philosopher, published the novel *The Ball and the Cross* in 1909 about two characters, a devout Christian and an ardent atheist, portrayed as the only sane men on the planet because they recognized the significance of their views and were willing to stand for their convictions. In his classic style, Chesterton contrasts "the ball" (the earth) with "the cross" (Christianity) to illustrate what he deems to be the only two viable options regarding ultimate reality. The world either points to itself or points beyond itself to a transcendent God.

When I speak of Nothing throughout this book, I do so in a manner similar to Chesterton's novel. The Nothing is a worldview that accepts the earth as an end in itself. This outlook is free from all religious beliefs and explanations. It is unhindered by divine revelation. It is untainted by church tradition. For many, it represents ultimate emancipation.

A great number of those who embrace this perspective work diligently to establish meaning and significance apart from God, and they are to be commended for their efforts. The term *Nothing* is not intended to trivialize their position. I've known many skeptics who live exemplary lives. And I have good friends, like Zach, who are secularists who are moral, kind, and thoughtful individuals.

Conversely, I've also known believers who don't live consistently with the very foundations they claim to embrace. Sadly, I need look no further for examples of this than to my own life. So this book isn't about who is the most moral or even the most intelligent. It's about the big decision every person must make in life. It's about the importance of this decision. And it's about the inevitability of making a choice between Jesus or Nothing.

I'm truly thankful for the bold vision of flourishing offered by many humanists today, yet, like Christian apologist Ravi Zacharias, I find it difficult to draw a logical connection between a secular worldview and the corresponding values. Zacharias provides a helpful description:

> Why don't we see more atheists like Jean Paul Sartre, or Friedrich Nietzsche, or Michel Foucault? These three philosophers, who also embraced atheism, recognized that in the absence of God, there was no transcendent meaning beyond one's own self-interests, pleasures, or tastes. . . . Without God, there is a crisis of meaning, and these three thinkers, among others, show us a world of just stuff, thrown out into space and time, going nowhere, meaning nothing.[2]

The recognition that apart from God there is a loss of transcendent meaning is central to the philosophy known as nihilism. I'll mention this outlook several times throughout this book. The term *nihilism* is based on the Latin word *nihil*, meaning "nothing." This is a view of reality that recognizes that the world by itself, apart from the existence of God, offers no intrinsic meaning or value.

Francis Schaeffer, the late Christian philosopher, believed that atheism and nihilism are inextricably connected. There are but two viable, mutually exclusive, ultimate worldview options: theism and nihilism. He contended that the logical conclusions of atheism are unlivable, forcing the secularist to live on capital borrowed from a theistic worldview.[3]

Schaeffer was not saying, and neither am I, that nonbelievers are immoral or unloving, but that their worldview commitments don't logically lead to the values they embrace. That's why Schaeffer said that humanists have their feet "firmly planted in midair"[4] because their understanding of reality does not establish a foundation capable of upholding their ideals.

Like Schaeffer, philosopher Alex Rosenberg sees atheism as leading inevitably to nihilism (though he prefers the nuanced term *nice nihilism*). In his book *The Atheist's Guide to Reality: Enjoying Life without Illusions*, Rosenberg offers a serious discussion of the implications of his *scientism* (a term he prefers over *atheism*). He describes scientism as a worldview that only accepts answers clearly provided by science.

Rosenberg understands that he cannot have his cake and eat it too. "When it comes to ethics, morality, and value," he writes, "we have to embrace an unpopular position that will strike many people as immoral as well as impious. So be it. . . . If you are going to be scientistic, you will have to be comfortable with a certain amount of nihilism.⁵" Though he recognizes that this conclusion presents some public relations challenges for atheism, he makes a case for embracing it nonetheless since "scientism can't avoid nihilism."[6]

While secular humanists will debate this point, readers must consider whether they are able to provide an *objective* basis for their perspectives. Protagoras, the early Greek philosopher, famously said, "Man is the measure of all things." This is something of a creed for humanism, yet it illustrates that apart from God our values become dangerously relative. Without God we can either look for subjective meaning within or search without for significance from an uncaring cosmos.

Philosophers aren't the only ones to recognize the loss of objective value in the absence of God. "We are more insignificant than we ever imagined," said Lawrence Krauss, celebrated theoretical physicist, at the 2009 meeting of the Atheist Alliance International. While Krauss's gift of humor makes his elaborate presentations entertaining, it doesn't make his conclusions any easier to swallow. He continues:

> If you take the universe—everything we see—stars and galaxies and clusters—everything we see: If you get rid of it, the universe is essentially the same. We constitute a one-percent bit of pollution in a universe that is thirty-percent dark matter and seventy-percent dark energy. We are completely irrelevant. Why such

a universe in which we're so irrelevant would be made for us is beyond me.[7]

I understand Krauss's point of how the scope of the universe makes our existence seem irrelevant, but what if we aren't the point of creation? For that matter, what if creation is not the point of creation? What if there is a Creator behind it all, and what if he is the ultimate point of all things? What if Krauss is reading the wrong story line? While it's worth considering the implications if Krauss's premise were right, what if he's not?

The Story of the Gospel

On the other hand, the gospel portrays each of us as a sort of mixed bag. We are both great and wretched. If the gospel is true, then we are created in the image of God. So that means we are not trivial despite our abysmally small size in comparison to the expanding universe. In fact, Scripture places humanity at the pinnacle, though not the center, of the created world with the important mandate to steward the earth.

Scripture frequently explains God's sovereignty with the reminder of his exclusive role in creation. Take the Old Testament example of Job: when faced with Job's accusations of unfairness, God simply asks Job where he happened to be on the day when the foundations of the world were established. The point is simple, and Job gets it: God is supreme above all created things.

Even though humans are the apex of creation, we are

not autonomous. God reigns supremely over all that he has made. In our depravity, however, we seek to move God out of his rightful position and assert ourselves as the sole authority of our lives.

While the gospel reveals our intrinsic value as the height of creation, it also shows the depth of our depravity through our multifaceted and ever-creative forms of mutiny. Humans are highly competent sinners. It doesn't take a rocket scientist to understand that we—like Adam and Eve—have a moral attraction for forbidden fruit and an aversion to moral accountability. Perhaps that's why the peaceful garden of Eden spans only two chapters in the biblical narrative. An earthly utopia is presented as a mere speed bump on the road to redemption.

Yet, the gospel offers hope for wandering hearts like ours. The Bible reveals that instead of judging all of humanity in one fell swoop—God visited us in our despair. The gospel is the story of God writing himself into human history. Of course, if God really does exist, then he has been a part of the story from the very beginning. Thus, the gospel is really not our introduction to God, but rather our re-introduction.

Christianity makes the unique claim that God actually entered the human theater to take on flesh and reassume the leading role (John 1). That is why the gospel is first and foremost a historical claim. If Jesus did not exist in real history, if he did not rise from the dead according to the Scriptures, then Christianity is false.

But how might reality be different if Jesus actually did (and still does) exist? What if the resurrection really happened? What if a relationship with God is in fact the most fulfilling experience any human can ever know? What if the gospel really is true?

In short, the gospel is the narrative of Christ's miraculous birth, perfect life, substitutionary death, and bodily resurrection. The holidays of Christmas and Easter form bookends in the story of Jesus summarized in the simple word *gospel*. "For God so loved the world," reads John 3:16, "that he gave his only Son, that whoever believes in him should not perish but have eternal life." That is the gospel in a nutshell. And it's either true or false.

The gospel does not enjoy a middle category immune from truth or falsehood, to be accepted only through a blind leap of faith. The gospel is a set of propositions about human history and ultimate reality. And it's not morally neutral. The gospel forces a decision, calling for repentance and faith in Christ. There is no middle ground. Every person must navigate the intellectual landscape between the competing worldviews of Jesus or Nothing.

If you are a Christian weighed down with uncertainty, or if you are a skeptic and you reject the claims of Jesus altogether, I hope you are willing to spend some time and invest the energy to consider the tale of these two stories. I know it would be the height of all hubris to think one short book could undo someone's deep-seated doubts. But what if your doubts are wrong?

The Wager between the Story Lines

This touches at the core of Pascal's famous "wager." Blaise Pascal was a seventeenth-century French mathematician, physicist, and philosopher. He is best remembered by the formula he framed for weighing the outcomes of belief or lack thereof. Pascal's wager offered two categorical options for humanity. And as a mathematician, Pascal ran the numbers and offered a basic conclusion: believing in God makes sense.

Consider this, if a Christian is wrong about the existence of a personal God, in death he or she will not know it. If the atheist is wrong and God does exist, then he or she will be fully aware of this error beyond the grave.

If it were a bet, the logical decision would be to believe in God. But most reasonable people don't want to gamble with issues as big as life, death, and eternity. Before you quickly dismiss Pascal's theory, however, you should understand that he was not looking for some kind of cheap religion.

Pascal is often criticized for making faith—as revealed in his wager—appear easy or flippant. Yet this is not at all the case. A complete reading of his work *Pensées*, French for "thoughts," clearly demonstrates that he considered deeply the issues of pleasure. Yet, like C. S. Lewis after him, he understood that the trouble with our desires is simply that they are too small. For Pascal, the gospel offers greater joy than can be found in earthly pursuits. And he was willing to stake his life on it.

"Pascal's argument should never be offered as a proof for God's existence," says Ravi Zacharias, "or as a reason for belief in him. This was never Pascal's intention."[8] Zacharias contends that Pascal's wager is one of the most misunderstood arguments in Christian apologetics. Pascal had a simple goal, according to Zacharias: "to meet only one challenge of atheism, and that is the test of existential self-fulfillment."[9]

Pascal's thoughts are all too often misconstrued, in my opinion, because they are considered in light of modern evangelistic gimmicks. I understand why some would consider the wager a call for mere intellectual assent, a philosophical version of the sinner's prayer—as if to say, "Just repeat after me and you'll be okay."

That's really not what Pascal had in mind though. The Stanford Encyclopedia of Philosophy provides a helpful clarification for such misunderstandings: "What Pascal intends by 'wagering for God' is an ongoing action—indeed, one that continues until your death—that involves your adopting a certain set of practices and living the kind of life that fosters belief in God."[10]

Pascal sought to demonstrate the power of the gospel to meet the human need for purpose and significance—and if true—to offer a great deal more. He was calling people to make a lifelong commitment to God that he believed would provide existential value for the human experience here and now and eternal value in the life to come.

This argument is far from a slam dunk with skeptics,

however. Giving up earthly pleasures for the sake of heavenly promises is not a trivial matter. Zach once asked me if my life is any different because I am a believer. A Christian student sitting nearby laughed and said, "Well, I certainly hope so!" The point Zach was making was much bigger than I even recognized at the time. And I didn't want to dismiss it as quickly as our friend did.

Zach was right. There is a moral component to believing in Jesus—it places a person firmly beneath a moral law with a moral Judge. This requires the denial of certain pleasures, and Zach's point was simply that becoming a Christian was not a morally neutral decision. If Christianity is false, then the believer has lived within a set of unnecessary constraints. In sum, as a Christian, I'm betting that my faith will yield a better return than forbidden fruit.

It's been over three centuries since Pascal's death, yet his arguments continue to permeate contemporary discussions about faith. It seems as though he touched a nerve that's still twitching beneath the surface of the human experience today. That's why I will borrow from his thoughts throughout the book.

Pascal's approach, however, is not uniquely religious. Singer and songwriter John Lennon once asked us to wager that God doesn't exist. He asked us to imagine a world without a heaven or a hell. Lennon offered a vision of an atheistic utopia. In the spirit of Pascal, I want to invert Lennon's request and invite you to consider what the world looks like when viewed through the lens of the gospel.

The gospel is the theist's guide to reality.

The following chapters will follow a simple pattern. I want to use the book of Colossians to contrast a gospel vision of the world with an atheistic one. I hope to show how Paul's short letter to a young church in a secular context addresses the basic questions common to humanity.

This book is neither a Bible commentary nor a philosophical treatise. Both my limited treatment of the biblical text and my broad description of atheism will surely elicit critiques. Yet, I have sought to be fair in my understanding of both. And I am convinced that life really boils down to these two categories. It's either the ball or the cross. It's either Jesus or Nothing.

The Gospel Offers an Explanation for Our Existence

> Nature has some perfections to show that she is the image of God, and some defects to show that she is only His image.
>
> Pascal[1]

When Zach visits his parents for the holidays, he still joins them for Sunday worship. Everyone is always happy to see him. Little has changed in his home church. Few know of his journey away from faith. Few understand the depth of his questions or the freedom he experienced in letting go of the idea of God.

The hymns, which he can't help but remember and even sing along to, ring a rather hollow note in comparison to his new outlook. Religion has its place. It serves as a kind of space holder for humankind's deepest longings. But it's just not true. These reservations pervade his thoughts as the pastor begins his sermon. Years ago the passion of the homily would stir him. Today it's nothing more than dogma dressed in bravado.

And it hits him afresh why he left it all behind. It seems so disconnected from reality. So myopic. So ignorant. So foolish.

There on the same uncomfortable wooden pew his family has always occupied, everything strikes him as strangely foreign. It's nearly dreamlike, the feelings of nostalgia mingled with déjà vu. Could it be that he has changed so much—or has he really felt this way all along? He now finds it hard to understand why any thinking person would persist in beliefs that are so clearly divorced from the real world.

Yet he knows that the notion of God as an ultimate explanation of origins is not easily avoided. The history of ideas is replete with intellectual leaders who possessed an unshakeable faith. Philosophy and science alike are rife with references to God. Even contemporary skeptical scholars find it difficult to avoid religious language when describing their grand theories.

This reminds me of an episode from my teen years. Twenty miles of interstate framed by corn and soybean fields separated my hometown from the nearest shopping mall. This commercialistic pilgrimage always sparked adolescent enthusiasm—for mostly good reasons—but I won't get into all of that. On this particular trip I was on a mission.

I was enamored with a certain scientific author, and I

wanted to be able to tell my friends I had read his books. This is of course a telltale sign of a pseudo-intellectual. Apparently I was not alone. The book, upon its initial release, was quickly christened "the least-read best seller." In my teenage hubris I thought I would be the exception.

Sitting cross-legged in the middle of the book aisle, my eyes glossing over, I tried reading Stephen Hawking's description of black holes in his book *A Brief History of Time*. As a seventeen-year-old I was clueless about general relativity and quantum theory. To be honest, I can't say I have a much better grasp on these concepts now. But one passage struck me as unusual—and I've returned to it many times since my adolescent years. In the final pages Hawking describes his quest to find a "theory of everything." He says that if we find such a theory, it will be complete, simple, and understandable:

> However, if we discover a complete theory, it should in time be understandable by everyone, not just by a few scientists. Then we shall all, philosophers, scientists and just ordinary people, be able to take part in the discussion of the question of why it is that we and the universe exist. If we find the answer to that, it would be the ultimate triumph of human reason—for then we should know the mind of God.[2]

Anyone familiar with Stephen Hawking as a scientist and author will know he is an atheist. He doesn't believe God is a rational explanation for anything. Yet his word choice is conspicuous because this is the central claim of the Christian message. If the gospel is true, then Christians do know the mind of God because he has revealed it to them.

The gospel is the Christian's theory of everything. As Francis Schaeffer said, "Christians should point out that there is no answer to these questions except that God is there and he is not silent. . . . It is this or nothing."[3] Schaeffer recognized the power of the gospel to explain the human experience. And he contended that the gospel's alternatives couldn't provide answers to humanity's perennial questions.

A theory of everything (often abbreviated TOE) must account for the sum total of what it means to be human. This is an ongoing obstacle for a materialistic view of the universe. The idea that everything must have a material explanation—with no reference to anything outside of nature—is under the relentless pressure of reality. We constantly live as though there is more to life than matter. Due to the New Atheists' commitment to philosophical materialism, they seem to have painted themselves into a corner with little to say on important aspects of humanity.

And though science has contributed much to our daily lives, most people are suspicious of the idea that science is our only source of knowledge. The famous atheistic philosopher Bertrand Russell once said, "What science cannot discover, mankind cannot know."[4] But most people care deeply about things they have not discovered through the scientific method, such as love, beauty, altruism, and even religious longing.

Must we conclude that everything nonscientific is really a delusion?

Prominent atheist Richard Dawkins offers his materialistic worldview in a captivating format for a younger audience in his children's book *The Magic of Reality*. But how does the sort of deterministic universe that Dawkins believes in call for the spark of grandeur with which he describes it? What is magical about a materialistic explanation of the cosmos that seems incapable of explaining the values that, for most of us, make life livable?

In contrast, Edgar H. Andrews, emeritus professor of materials at the University of London, highlights theism's ability to account for the nonmaterial. Andrews suggests, "A true 'theory of everything,' therefore, must embrace both material and non-material aspects of the universe, and my contention is that we already possess such a theory, namely, the hypothesis of God."[5]

If theism is true, then it surely provides a more complete account of the human epic, explaining both the material that is immediately available to our senses and the immaterial stuff that we all care about so much, but cannot examine under a microscope or through a telescope.

The Colossians Quotient:
The Gospel as a Christian Theory of Everything

The apostle Paul presents the gospel as a comprehensive explanation of humanity's history and a reliable guide for the future. Paul preached Christ as the ultimate explanation for both the material and the nonmaterial, from the origin of the universe to our moral inclinations. Consider the radical implications of his words in the first chapter of Colossians:

> He is the image of the invisible God, the firstborn of all creation. For by him all things were created, in heaven and on earth, visible and invisible, whether thrones or dominions or rulers or authorities—all things were created through him and for him. And he is before all things, and in him all things hold together. And he is the head of the body, the church. He is the beginning, the firstborn from the dead, that in everything he might be preeminent. For in him all the fullness of God was pleased to dwell, and through him to reconcile to himself all things, whether on earth or in heaven, making peace by the blood of his cross. (Col. 1:15–20)

This is a bold declaration of the explanatory power of the gospel. Similarly, the twentieth-century British author Dorothy Sayers recognized the power of the gospel to explain our existence: "It is fatal to let people suppose that Christianity is only a mode of feeling; it is vitally necessary to insist that it is first and foremost a rational explanation of the universe."[6] If the gospel is true, then Christ *is* the basis for understanding *everything*.

Consider the scope of the gospel's explanation. The gospel reveals why there is something rather than nothing, where the universe came from, why it is orderly, why humanity is personal, and why we long for transcendence.

Christ made all things visible and invisible. If the gospel is true, the scope of its explanatory power is boundless.

In Colossians, Paul explains that Jesus, the icon of God, is the Creator and Sustainer of all things. All the promises of Scripture are contingent upon these facts that God created the world and that he has visited us in our suffering. In this way, the gospel unites the incarnation with the creation. Both are crucial for a Christian theory of everything. These truths are foundational for Christianity. Jesus is central to the explanation of everything, from beginning to end.

The origin of the universe is the focal point of the opening chapters of the Bible, which reveal that God created the world out of nothing (Gen. 1:1). This is very different from the atheistic claim that something has come from nothing. Instead of nothing causing everything, or even some sort of impersonal matter as the source of all things, the Bible explains that the universe is the result of an infinite mind.

The Bible's opening verses reveal the Spirit of God hovering over the face of the waters in the midst of a dark cosmos. This silence is broken by God's declaration, "Let there be light" (Gen. 1:2–3). The Old Testament, which begins with creation, ends with Israel's final prophet, Malachi. His ministry was followed by a bleak period in Jewish history. There were no word from God and no prophets for hundreds of years.

The Old Testament begins in physical darkness and ends in spiritual darkness. This silent interlude between the Old and New Testaments was interrupted when John the Baptist entered the scene as a voice in the wilderness declaring the way of the Lord. He served a pivotal role in breaking the spiritual darkness.

John was not the true light, but he came to testify of the true light. In this way, the Gospels offer a parallel to the opening verses of the Old Testament, particularly in the genesis of Jesus's public ministry inaugurated at his baptism. There the Spirit descended upon him and God the Father declared, "This is my beloved Son, with whom I am well pleased" (Matt. 3:17).

In the midst of this spiritual darkness, God's Spirit again descended upon the face of the waters. And the voice of God was once again heard in Israel. The apostle Paul explicitly connects the creation and the incarnation: "For God, who said, 'Let light shine out of darkness,' has shone in our hearts to give the light of the knowledge of the glory of God in the face of Jesus Christ" (2 Cor. 4:6). Here, Paul bonds the Genesis account with the gospel itself. The God who commanded light to shine (Genesis 1) once again penetrated the darkness (John 1).

But there is more. This light, Paul says, has shone in the hearts of those who believe. This is the existential reality of the Christian faith: the light of God spoken at the creation of the cosmos has resounded throughout the corridors of human history, manifestly in the person of Jesus, and now fills the life of the believer.

The Christian account of reality can be summarized with these four words: *creation*, *separation*, *incarnation*, and *regeneration*. God has revealed himself in creation and in the Son so that we might experience a new birth. This is the basic message of the gospel. And this is Paul's point in the first chapter of Colossians.

The God who created the universe has visited his creation to make "peace through the blood of his cross." The reference to the cross making peace illustrates the reality of the existence of evil. Paul says later in chapter 2 that God has triumphed over the rulers of spiritual darkness through the cross (Col. 2:15). Thus, the incarnation is the dawn of God's kingdom and the dusk of Satan's reign.

Creative Alternatives

In our day, however, many people aren't interested in an explanation of the origins of the universe that involves miracles and demons. Competing concepts to the creation account are given a lot more attention in the marketplace of ideas. One hypothesis that has received a lot of press is the "multiverse theory." This is the concept that there are an infinite number of randomly ordered universes that through some sort of cosmic natural selection have produced a cosmos capable of sustaining human life.

If there are billions and billions of worlds, the theory goes, then there is no need for references to God to explain the intricate design in our universe that makes life possible. Who needs the supernatural if a satisfactory natural explanation is available? But this theory only pushes the problem back a step, or an infinite number of steps it seems, forcing the question, Who created all the other universes?

For those who place a premium on scientific evidence, it is a little surprising that a theory like this, with absolutely no empirical evidence, is received so warmly. But regardless of how many universes we might imagine, we still must account for how mere matter produced beings like us. Pushing the first domino back further doesn't solve the question of origins or the riddle of humanity.

Let me offer an illustration. American football games always begin with a coin toss. The team captain from the away team gets to call heads or tails. If he gets it right, he gets to choose whether his team kicks or receives the ball. Now imagine a particular home team has won every coin toss for the last twenty years. This would be statistically improbable to absurd proportions, and the team as well as its midfield turf would come under investigation.

What if this team's head coach offered an argument like the following? "There really isn't a problem. It's all coincidence. You just need to think of our twenty years of winning consecutive coin tosses in the context of an infinite number of possible coin tosses. Given an infinite number of tosses, our string of wins really isn't so unlikely or impossible after all."

Most people would want to examine the cumulative evidence surrounding the coin tosses before they would consider a complex philosophical theory. The whole thing looks rigged. And just thinking about it in light of an infinite number of possibilities doesn't make the situation appear any less suspect. The head coach shouldn't get an easy pass using his argument, and neither should popular atheistic authors.

The same is true for theories about our universe. That's why Sir Fred Hoyle, considered to be one of the most distinguished and controversial scientists of the twentieth century, once said, "A common sense interpretation of the facts suggests that a superintellect has monkeyed with the physics."[7] Like the coin-toss example, before we reach for intricate theories about infinite possibilities, it might be prudent first to consider if our universe has been "monkeyed with" by a "superintellect." The facts seem to point that way.

But not everyone is willing to entertain the notion that our world could be the product of a designer. Perhaps that's one of the reasons why atheistic authors like Richard Dawkins and Laurence Krauss advance the multiverse theory. It attempts to negate the need for references to the supernatural. But it only pushes the problem back further. And I'm not sure it passes what Christian apologist Greg Koukl calls the "So what?" test.

Let's concede, for the moment, that there are infinite other universes that we can't see even through our most powerful telescopes. We will just accept (by faith) that they exist. And furthermore, let's assume that somehow these universes produced our planet with its delicate design providing for intelligent and personal life.

So what?

How does this solve the problem? How did the countless other universes come into existence? This still doesn't account for how personality, purpose, and meaning can come from eternal, mindless, and impersonal matter.

Billions of universes? Okay, but so what?

Ironically, in the end the multiple universe theory is an unavoidably religious claim itself. While I doubt Dawkins will become an ordained minister of the "Church of the Multiverse," he has placed himself firmly within his own criticisms by adopting views that are devoid of physical evidence.

Creation is either the result of an eternal, personal, and intelligent being or the accidental effect of eternal, impersonal, and mindless matter with unknowable origins. It should be the life quest of every responsible and thinking individual to determine which account of the cosmos best answers the ultimate questions and sufficiently accounts for our day-to-day lives.

Could the gospel, if true, provide a comprehensive way to understand our world and ourselves? John Polkinghorne, former professor of mathematical physics at Cambridge University, thinks so. He summarized this view by saying, "I believe that Christianity affords a coherent insight into the strange way the world is."[8] The Christian "theory of everything" offers an explanation for why we, as relational beings, live in an orderly universe. The idea of an intelligent Creator does not conflict with reality but rather offers a "coherent insight" into our strange world.

Understanding the creation, and more importantly the Creator, is foundational for a theory of everything.

He Is There and He Is Not Silent

The hypothesis of God provides, at least for many, a convincing explanation of origins. Even unbelievers recognize it as a force to be reckoned with. There is a telling scene in the documentary *Collision* featuring the book and debate tour between late atheistic journalist Christopher Hitchens and evangelical pastor Doug Wilson. The scene comes at the end of the production when Wilson asks "Hitch" what argument for God's existence is the most problematic. Hitchens quickly responds that there is something of a consensus among atheists he knows that it is the apparent fine-tuning of the universe.

In fact, it was arguments from design that the late philosopher Antony Flew originally rejected as an atheistic student at Oxford University. He presented his arguments at the Socratic Club, a student forum for dialogues about Christianity, led by none other than C. S. Lewis.[9] By the end of Flew's life, however, it was ultimately the intricate design in the universe that led him to renounce his atheism and publish the book *There Is a God: How the World's Most Notorious Atheist Changed His Mind*.

The design implications led Flew only to a form of deism, however, with a god who exists but who has not revealed himself. While theists have celebrated Flew's transformation, he clearly stopped short of the gospel. It seems to be a limitation of arguments from design that they can only lead to some sort of deism. A god who is merely the creator is unable to solve the puzzle of the human experience.

Only the gospel can lead us *further up and further in*. That's why the Christian should seek to counter alternative worldviews not with an unknowable god but with Christ himself. While theism provides a compelling explanation of reality, it falls dreadfully short without the gospel.

Theism best explains reality: Jesus best explains theism.

That's why the gospel is a complete worldview; it explains both the outer world of creation and the inner world of human experience. Engraved on the tombstone of philosopher Immanuel Kant are these memorable words: "Two things never cease to amaze me. The starry skies above me and the moral law within me."[10] The gospel shows how both find their source and substance in Christ. The incarnation makes theism tangible.

A silent god cannot account for the existence of evil. Antony Flew's deism could only claim that whatever is, is fine and good. Neither deism nor atheism has a category for objective evil. That's why a principal problem for such worldviews is the human desire to call things evil. When we are left without categories for moral distinctions, our moral repugnance loses all meaning. In deism god doesn't care, and in atheism the universe doesn't care.

As Alex Rosenberg states: "Reality is rough. But it could have been worse. We could have been faced with reality in all its roughness plus a God who made it that way."[11]

Deism only complicates the situation by adding a first cause to the beginning of time who is unable to help us in our day-to-day lives. Both atheism and deism result in a functionally godless cosmos with no basis for hope for a human narrative plagued by pain and suffering.

But let's consider another scenario. What if the world was indeed created good, but something has gone seriously wrong? And what if the Creator was willing to suffer with us, even for us, in order to make it right? What if it was once good—really good—but now we, through our rebellion, live with the knowledge of both good and evil? And deep inside of us we have a longing for someone to make things good again.

It seems that all of our great stories point this way. They all voice our yearning for redemption from the suffering in our world. Our most beloved epics usually center on a heroic figure who makes the ultimate sacrifice to purchase our liberation. From apocalyptic films like *I Am Legend* to historical fiction like *Saving Private Ryan* there is something about redemptive themes that resonates with humanity. And this is the paradoxical yet precious claim of the Christian narrative: God has entered time and space to suffer in our place.

The apostle Paul describes the incarnation in this way: "For in him all the fullness of God was pleased to dwell, and through him to reconcile to himself all things, whether on earth or in heaven, making peace by the blood of his cross" (Col. 1:19–20). Christ's sacrificial work obtained a means of reconciliation between the Creator and the created. Herein we find a clue for understanding our cosmos.

In Christ we find both an explanation of and a remedy for the evil in our world.

As a young man C. S. Lewis discovered that atheism didn't provide a compelling explanation of evil. In fact, Lewis reasoned, in the absence of God there can be no objective basis for justice. As a skeptic, Lewis argued against God that "the universe seemed so cruel and unjust."[12] Yet he realized he had no standard by which to call something cruel or unjust apart from an absolute source (i.e., God). His aversion to evil necessitated a standard of perfection that could only be found in God.

In short, Lewis's atheistic narrative was unable to support his assault against the divine. He was thus faced with the alternative of either giving up his idea of justice or surrendering to belief in God. He knew he couldn't cling to one without conceding the other. Or he could simply let go of both. He knew he couldn't have it both ways.

Lewis recognized that if he marginalized justice as a "private idea," then his "argument against God collapsed too."[13] He understood that "the whole of reality was senseless," but that he was "forced to assume that one part of reality—namely my idea of justice—was full of sense."[14] In other words, he had to first accept the existence of God in order to establish an argument against his existence. It was a self-defeating experience in logic.

This internal contradiction contributed to his trajectory toward faith. He would go on to reject atheism as "too simple" and unable to account for the human experience. Lewis's first step was out of the atheistic world and into the theistic one. Theism, however, proved to be insufficient. Lewis perceived the undeniable and pervasive evil in the world to be the principal obstacle for a theistic outlook—though he felt atheism failed to provide an adequate answer as well. This mystery could only be resolved by the gospel.

He found in the gospel both an explanation and a remedy for evil. Only a powerful and personal God could provide both. And thus Lewis's journey culminated in Christ. But this is not to suggest that it was (or is) an easy intellectual or volitional commitment.

Scripture reveals that God has created human beings in his own image and for his own glory. Yet humanity seeks fulfillment apart from God and exalts the creation rather than the Creator, receiving guilt and isolation instead of satisfaction and fulfillment. People's attempts to fill the void created by God's absence continue to prove futile. Pascal describes this reality:

> What is it, then, that this desire and this inability proclaim to us, but that there was once in man a true happiness of which there now remain to him only the mark and empty trace, which he in vain tries to fill from all his surroundings, seeking from things absent the help he does not obtain in things present? But these are

all inadequate, because the infinite abyss can only be filled by an infinite and immutable object, that is to say, only by God Himself.[15]

Humanity's search for an ultimate theory apart from God is as old as time itself. According to the Bible, it all began in a garden in the Middle East. Among the beauty of Eden a snake once whispered in the ear of Eve that he possessed a theory of everything. This proposition has manifested itself in various forms throughout the centuries, blinding the hearts of men and women from seeing the glory of God (2 Cor. 4:4).

Even as a teenager in a mall bookstore I sensed the power of the gospel to answer Stephen Hawking's search for truth. Apart from divine intervention the most brilliant of scientists will spend the sum of their days in search of a unifying theory. But if the gospel is true, then we really do know the mind of God: he has revealed it to us in creation, in his Word, and in his Son. And, if it is true, in this story we will understand *our* story.

3

The Gospel Offers Clarity
for Our Confusion

We desire truth, and find within ourselves only
uncertainty.

Pascal[1]

A student once approached me after I finished sharing the
gospel with her and a group of other university students.
She was a new convert, having been a Christian for only
three months. She was seeking to understand, as a major
in mathematics, how the gospel might fit within her discipline. She asked if we could talk for a moment. Her confusion was as clear to me as was her critique. She encouraged
me to stop saying that the gospel is true.

Was it because she really didn't believe the gospel? No.
I'm convinced, as much as I suppose I can be, that she had
experienced an authentic conversion. She was trying to
integrate my sermon with her college professor's words.

Her teacher had told her to never say that anything is absolutely true.

I'm not sure, however, that most students are equally skeptical about finding truth. Many students, like Zach, don't subscribe to the same sort of squishy relativism this student seemed to struggle with. Zach sees through the principle problems of postmodern thought. Yet, the idea that Christians "have all the answers" has always struck him as highly arrogant and intellectually lazy. He's always been irritated by the notion that the gospel speaks to every scientific quandary.

But let's zoom back a little and look, not at specific, detailed scientific claims, but at the bigger picture of truth in general and our ability to get at it. Is truth—the rock solid kind you anchor your life upon, the never changing, unconditional kind—is such truth even possible apart from God? Apart from the gospel can we really expect to find any kind of certainty? What are our options?

The Colossians Quotient: The Possibility of Certainty

Culture offers competing explanations to the biggest questions faced by humanity. That's why Paul's letter to the Colossians is foundational for understanding a Christian response to pluralistic truth options. Paul's thesis is clear enough: "I say this in order that no one may delude you with plausible arguments" (Col. 2:4). Paul recognized the gospel's place within a pluralistic society.

First, note both what Paul did and did not say. He did

not call the Colossians' attackers or their arguments stupid. He did not demean or condescend upon their intelligence. Rather, he said their arguments were "plausible." It appears that in Colossae the believers were exposed to what must have been widely accepted, apparently rational, and seemingly logical challenges to their faith.

Paul didn't panic. He showed them that while plausible, these arguments were still false. Paul expressed full confidence in the power of the gospel to equip believers in their stand for truth in the midst of a secular environment.

Like those in Colossae, Christians will face intellectual opposition. Our world is replete with rival claims, some more plausible than others. That is why believers and unbelievers alike should navigate the path from plausibility to certainty with intellectual caution.

Something from Nothing?

Let's try to unpack this by looking at a recent book that claims to solve the greatest philosophical quandary known to humanity: *A Universe from Nothing: Why There Is Something Rather Than Nothing*, by Lawrence Krauss, published in 2012. Krauss offers a finely tuned argument against the idea of God as a necessary first cause, or as an explanation to why the universe, or anything for that matter, exists.

Krauss is not entirely reckless in his claims. He often uses language marked by caution and humility. "I stress the word could here," Krauss writes, "because we may never have enough empirical information to resolve this question unambiguously. But the fact that a universe from nothing is even plausible is certainly significant, at least to me."[2] Though space is limited, let's consider his "plausible" claim.

For this exercise, we will use a *New York Times* review of Krauss's book to help illustrate how one reviewer, David Albert, analyzes Krauss's arguments. I'll emphasize only a few highlights and try to keep the otherwise technical discussion simple.

David Albert, professor of philosophy at Columbia University, offers a few candid critiques of *A Universe from Nothing*. First, he notes that Krauss uses the term *nothing* in a misleading way. When Krauss talks about nothing, he is referring to the quantum vacuum. If you don't understand much about quantum vacuums, don't be discouraged; you are not alone. Just keep in mind that when Krauss talks about the "nothing" from which he says the entire world came, he is talking about this vacuum. Whether or not it should truly be called "nothing" is open to debate.

And that is exactly what happened when Christian apologist William Lane Craig and Lawrence Krauss faced off on the campus of North Carolina State University to discuss the existence of God. Craig took issue with Krauss's use of the term *nothing*, charging Krauss with a "grossly misleading use of the 'nothingness' for describing the quantum vacuum" since the vacuum, as Craig explained, is "a rich, physical reality described by physical laws and having a physical structure."[3]

To be fair to Krauss, in public talks he has admitted

that when he talks about nothing, he really doesn't mean nothing, but rather, a "bubbling, broiling, brew of virtual particles."[4] So even if we concede that the quantum vacuum should be called "nothing," we still must ask, Where did this brew of virtual particles come from? It seems that nothing might be better described as something.

It reminds me of a comment I once heard from a skeptic friend who said, "We know the universe came from nothing, or at least from very little." But wait a minute; isn't there a vast difference between the two? Which is it? Did the universe come from nothing or from very little? Krauss doesn't really differentiate between nothing and very little in his book, but uses the term *nothing* to describe elements that seem like, well, something. But let's move on.

Furthermore, where did the laws that govern the nothing come from? This is another point of critique offered by Albert—that Krauss assumes the existence of the laws of quantum mechanics. Again, you don't need a degree in quantum mechanics to understand this point. Simply put, if we accept Krauss's definition of *nothing*, we still haven't explained where the natural laws come from that have guided nothing into creating everything.

What are the origins of these laws? In a parenthetical statement toward the end of his book Krauss simply admits that the laws of quantum mechanics must be assumed.[5] Okay. Let's just assume them and keep moving.

But first, let's summarize a little bit. The universe was created by nothing, according to Krauss. The nothing isn't really nothing, but is actually a bubbling, broiling, brew of virtual particles. Krauss doesn't explain where this brew came from. And as for the laws that govern the bubbling brew, well, we're not really sure where they came from either.[6]

So how plausible do you find the claim that Krauss has solved the mystery of the age-old question, Why is there something rather than nothing?

A final and deeper critique offered by Albert is that Krauss's book is really a heavy-handed attack on religion. Albert closes his analysis with these words: "It seems like a pity, and more than a pity, and worse than a pity . . . to think that all that gets offered to us now, by guys like these, in books like this, is the pale, small, silly, nerdy accusation that religion is, I don't know, *dumb*."[7] Perhaps this is the most fundamental charge against Krauss's book: that it is contempt for religion cloaked in scientific theory.

Please understand that I am not foolhardy enough to believe I have successfully negated an award-winning theoretical physicist in these few short paragraphs. I cannot even pronounce some of the words in Krauss's book, to be totally honest. He is an expert in his field and a really smart guy. Yet, what I do hope I have demonstrated is the importance of thinking critically about such plausible claims. Perhaps Krauss has deeper commitments that are guiding his ostensibly scientific conclusions.

All too often I hear of college students who speak of such theories as being factual. Sadly, the leap from plausibility to certainty is often taken uncritically. That's why I like to help students apply caution in navigating the intellectual landscape of contemporary truth claims like those offered by Lawrence Krauss.

Peeling the Onion

Something I like to do with my students in my intro to philosophy courses is ask them to define truth. My goal is to help them develop a critical mind so that they can analyze the various claims they hear on a regular basis. All too often conversations about important and controversial topics become conquests in sheer determination. They can quickly devolve into intellectual dodgeball competitions with participants hurling sound bites at one another. I like to use the metaphor of an onion to illustrate the process of evaluating arguments (see fig. 1).

Figure 1

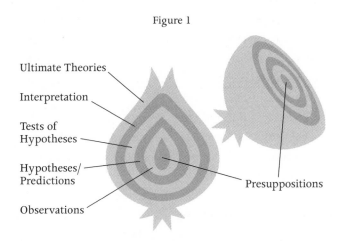

Ultimate Theories

Interpretation

Tests of
Hypotheses

Hypotheses/
Predictions

Observations

Presuppositions

The outer layer of the onion represents the participants' ultimate theories or worldviews. The next layer down contains their various interpretations and attempts to synthesize all the information they feel is important. When you peel this layer back, you find different empirical or philosophical tests they have observed in order to try out their hypotheses and predictions about how the world works. Their working hypotheses (informed guesses) and predictions belong to the next layer and are based on their general observations of the world around them. Their observations represent the final layer of the onion.

I present the onion metaphor to assist students in moving an argument beyond the initial presentation of a given theory. I intentionally leave the most important detail out until the end. Then, if I'm drawing the illustration on the board, I sketch the core of the onion and write to the side, "Presuppositions." These are assumptions that people make about the world that predate their actual observations. Presuppositions are beliefs people accept apart from empirical evidence. They function as a lens through which evidence is screened and interpreted.

It is important to note that most of us don't really begin with the observations and hypotheses. We rely heavily upon experts, and for a lot of good reasons. First, we don't have time, energy, and resources to do the research that is necessary. Second, why recreate the wheel? We really don't need to start over and ignore centuries of intellectual labor.

But what if we too quickly accept certain interpretations and conclusions that are heavily influenced and shaped by the experts' presuppositions? It could be that something is only deemed plausible because it lines up with one's prior commitments. That's why we need to be careful about blindly accepting conclusions without considering the underpinning presuppositions.

The most fundamental presupposition is one's view of God. Because the existence of God cannot ultimately be proved or disproved by scientific data, it is by definition a presupposition. This is not to say that there are not good reasons to believe in God. However, belief in God, or lack thereof, is something that one must presuppose about the world. And it's the most foundational aspect of someone's worldview. The question to consider is, Which intellectual commitment does reality seem to support?

This is perhaps something that Zach understands in a different way than many of his college peers. Some of his friends were raised in Christian homes, and still hold to their Christian faith; some of them were raised in secular homes and continue to disbelieve in God. Unlike them, Zach has seen both sides. But what strikes him from time to time is how intelligent people on either side of the God equation can look at the same data and come to such different conclusions.

The Core of Presuppositions

This is because no one comes to the scientific method from a neutral vantage point. As atheistic philosopher Daniel Dennett said, "There is no such thing as philosophy-free science; there is only science whose philosophical baggage is taken on board without examination."[8] And as Albert Einstein once observed, "The man of science is a poor philosopher."[9] This is why it is crucial to analyze arguments or theories in order to examine the philosophical baggage behind any apparent plausibility.

John Lennox, professor of mathematics at Oxford University, makes this clear: "Admitting our biases is the best way towards rational discussion which I would welcome."[10] Lennox recognizes that he brings his belief in God to the scientific method. And he knows that admitting this bias up front will help him be a better scientist.

Richard Lewontin, Harvard University emeritus professor of biology, an atheist, has made an equally transparent concession. In an article published by the *New York Review of Books* in January 1997, Lewontin admits that his atheistic view of the world is not based on scientific investigation. He accepts, as a prior commitment, that there is no God. He also says that a materialistic view of reality must be considered absolute in order to prevent a "Divine Foot in the door."[11]

Both Lennox and Lewontin appear forthright in placing their presuppositions on the table. Many are not nearly as transparent or self-aware. This is one reason why universities actually require postgraduate students to state their biases up front when writing a doctoral dissertation. If biases are unknown, unrecognized, or simply denied, they will prevent a meaningful pursuit of truth and could taint any conclusions based on the research.

Whenever I read the apostle Paul's reference in Colossians to plausible arguments, I'm reminded of the power of presuppositions and how they undergird everything we do. If you want to evaluate someone's position, it is helpful to begin by looking at the person's fundamental worldview commitments. Where someone begins will often determine where he or she will end.

Deceptive Philosophy

Later in the second chapter of Colossians Paul uses stronger language to describe the secular challenges of the day, giving emphasis to the nature of misleading philosophy. Instead of describing such arguments as plausible, he says they are intended to deceive: "See to it that no one takes you captive by philosophy and empty deceit, according to human tradition, according to elemental spirits of the world, and not according to Christ" (Col. 2:8).

This change of tone is also seen in Paul's words of caution. He begins with an imperative, "See to it." This statement is intended to express urgency and elicit a response. He places the Colossians on high alert.

In the spring of 2012 the town I live in, Louisville, Kentucky, became the focus of meteorologists across the nation because of a powerful storm front. I remember reading on Twitter about an anchorman from the Weather Channel who had flown into town earlier that afternoon to cover the storm. That's never a good sign.

When the local stations changed the tornado *watch* to

a tornado *warning*, our entire city took cover. A tornado watch simply means the conditions are right for a tornado. A warning means a tornado has touched down in the area. While Louisville was largely unaffected, the towns of Henryville and Marysville, Indiana, just nineteen miles to the north, were devastated.

As in the severe weather example, the apostle Paul was not issuing a watch to the Colossians. His severe words denote a warning. An intellectual F4 tornado was ripping a trail through Colossae, and Paul was telling believers to be prepared. He knew too well the devastation of dangerous ideas.

Paul encouraged believers to find shelter in the gospel. He expressed full confidence that in it they could withstand any storm. That's why he later commended them for their faith, which he described as "rooted and built up," "established," and "abounding in thanksgiving" (Col. 2:7). The gospel offers a safe haven for all weather-weary travelers in search of certainty. But can the same sort of assurance be found apart from God? Can science alone establish a foundation for knowledge?

The Gospel Makes Reason Reasonable

The discipline of modern science blossomed in the fertile soil of a Christian worldview.[12] The iconic scientist Isaac Newton, a believer, expected his study of nature to provide insights into reality. But why did he place such faith in the scientific process? Because he believed discoverable laws ordered the universe, and because he held the conviction that humanity, made in the image of God, possessed the reliable mental aptitude for discovering and discerning truth.

This confidence about the world and about our ability to grasp truth was basic to the scientific endeavor. But what would happen if we lost our trust in both the orderliness of the universe and the reliability of our own minds? How might our enthusiasm for pursuing truth be dampened or diminished?

In atheism, for example, should humans be optimistic that they possess the mental ability to establish a reliable understanding of the world? Even Charles Darwin seemed to share this concern in a letter he penned to William Graham regarding Graham's book *The Creed of Science: Religious, Moral and Social*:

> With me the horrid doubt always arises whether the convictions of man's mind, which has been developed from the mind of the lower animals, are of any value or at all trustworthy. Would any one trust in the convictions of a monkey's mind, if there are any convictions in such a mind?[13]

If our mind is itself the result of nonintelligent processes, then how can we be confident it is reliable? Alvin Plantinga, emeritus professor of philosophy at the University of Notre Dame, suggests that on this basis evolution actually disproves atheism. Plantinga, who accepts the basic tenets of evolution, believes that God is necessary to guide the process.

On the other hand, if the entire show is the result of blind chance, then there really is no reason to trust our mental faculties—which are just one small part of the show. If our brain is itself an accident, then any argument we develop to the contrary can only be considered just another accident. Any response, no matter how well articulated, to avoid this conclusion, must come from our brain and fall under the same shadow of doubt.

Atheistic philosophers recognize this challenge as well. In 2012, Thomas Nagel, professor of philosophy and law at New York University, published his controversial book *Mind and Cosmos: Why the Materialist Neo-Darwinian Conception of Nature Is Almost Certainly False*. In it he agrees with Plantinga's argument (simplified above), but he refuses to accept God as an ultimate explanation. So, while his book affirms the necessity of some sort of mind behind the universe, he refuses to say what that intelligence might actually be.

Why would Nagel recognize the problem of the materialistic outlook, yet refuse to accept a theistic worldview? It all seems to go back to presuppositions. In an earlier book, *The Last Word*, published in 1999, Nagel made this telling statement: "It isn't just that I don't believe in God and, naturally, hope that I'm right in my belief. It's that I hope there is no God! I don't want there to be a God; I don't want the universe to be like that."[14] His values and his worldview commitments seem to be in conflict now. Perhaps, we've not heard the *last word* from him on this subject.

It is extremely interesting, at least to me, how the gospel provides a basis both for our longing for truth and for the confidence we place in our mind's ability to comprehend it. The gospel has a funny way of explaining life and fitting it all together. It provides a foundation not only for a reasonable explanation of the universe, but also for a reasonable explanation of reason itself.

That's why I wasn't scandalized by the college student's request for me to quit saying the gospel is true. She was passionate about her faith but was struggling to synthesize Christianity within her academic discipline. I was reminded of the words of Nancy Pearcey: "Thinking Christianly means understanding that Christianity gives the truth about the whole of reality, a perspective for interpreting every subject matter."[15] Thus, the gospel is not one more fact to be synthesized, but a foundation for knowledge itself.

So, if the gospel is *true*, then we have a basis for *truth*. And furthermore, if it is true, then our confidence is not based merely on a theory but is grounded in a historical person. If Jesus is indeed the Way, the Truth, and the Life, then certainty *certainly* seems within our grasp after all. And if Jesus is indeed the Way, as he claimed to be, then we might even find rest for our weary souls.

The Gospel Offers Grace for Our Guilt

> The only thing which consoles us for our miseries is diversion, and yet this is the greatest of our miseries. For it is this which principally hinders us from reflecting upon ourselves and which makes us insensibly ruin ourselves.
>
> Pascal[1]

One thing Zach doesn't miss about religion is the constant use of guilt as a tool to motivate the masses. Yet the idea of grace, while somewhat disconnected from his personal experience in church, is one of the more attractive features of the Christian message. The idea of receiving a blank slate—total forgiveness—is something he even still wishes for at times.

I believe part of the reason for this is that deep down everyone is plagued by the dark reality of moral guilt. We carry within ourselves a stubborn sense that we have offended some cosmic order and that on a very practical level we don't always "do unto others as we would have them do unto us." It is as though there is some sort of higher standard that we all fall short of reaching. C. S. Lewis calls this the "Moral Law"[2] and describes it as the thing that seeks to govern our impulses.

Let me illustrate it in this way: Imagine you were to witness an elderly woman being robbed at knifepoint. Your "fight or flight" instincts would quickly kick in. Your heart would beat rapidly. Adrenaline would flood your system. Yet above these more basic reactions to run or resist, another impulse would arise, something seemingly superior altogether. This third impulse would actually seek to regulate which route of action you chose. And it would almost always, as Lewis points out, compel you to do the difficult thing: the heroic or sacrificial thing.

Yet it is the third impulse that we often ignore, preferring to follow instincts that are more self-gratifying or self-preserving. And in such choices, as much as we might dislike or try to deny it, we feel a sense of guilt or shame. It is as though we have a moral intuition that tells us we have missed the mark and that we should have chosen a more selfless option.

This reminds me of the television show *What Would You Do?*, with the ABC host John Quinones. Cameras are set up and a situation is created that forces an unknowing participant to make a moral decision. It's always touching to see those who make the right choice. And it's a little sad to watch people who opt to ignore whatever unfortunate event is playing out before them. And this is to say nothing of alternative situations where we actively choose to do the wrong thing. Our temptations come to us in the forms of both omission and commission.

Now imagine having cameras on you twenty-four hours a day, seven days a week, that captured every incident where you were forced to choose between right and wrong. You might object and say, "Who determines right and wrong?" But this objection ends when someone punches you in the nose, or rear ends your automobile, or fails to give you accurate change at the coffee shop.

We know there is a code, however nebulous we might say it is. And we know we don't perfectly keep it. And we are certainly offended when someone breaks the code in a way that affects us personally. So where might we find help navigating this code, and where might we find relief for our deep feeling that we are out of sorts with this higher standard?

I'm reminded of a trip to Britain I took with a friend in the summer of 2009 to speak at a youth event. We arrived a day early to do some sightseeing. We spent nearly two hours wandering the streets of London in search of an elusive burial ground. No one we met along the way could offer helpful directions. Then, finally, we saw a statue of John Wesley, over fifteen feet tall and bearing the inscription "The world is my parish." We had found the landmark we had desperately searched for, here in front of the church where Wesley served as pastor, and directly across from the cemetery we wished to visit.

Named Bunhill Fields, it is a dissenters' cemetery, a graveyard used for Protestants who claimed independence from the Church of England. This small cemetery is filled with historical giants, like hymn writer Isaac Watts, poet William Blake, Puritan author John Owen, to mention only a few. But there was one grave I was primarily interested in visiting.

The cemetery attendant unlocked a small gate allowing us passage to the tomb of John Bunyan, author of *The Pilgrim's Progress*. My mind is indelibly marked by images from this story as it was read to me in childhood. I had no idea two of the most captivating scenes from the book would be illustrated in the stone of Bunyan's tomb.

On one side of the mausoleum is an image from the opening scenes of *The Pilgrim's Progress*, in which the pilgrim is fleeing from the city of destruction. He leaves his family and friends behind as he embarks on a quest to find relief from the heavy burden affixed to his back. He encounters diverse personalities along the way—among them, Obstinate, Pliable, and Mr. Worldly Wiseman—but none can free him from his heavy load.

When I walked to the opposite side of Bunyan's tomb, I experienced a stab of joy. It portrayed the beautiful scene of the pilgrim finally finding liberation. When he ascended the top of a hill and knelt at the cross, his burden immediately fell off of his back and rolled into an open sepulcher never to be seen again. This is a gripping depiction of what it means to receive grace.

Guilt's Progeny: Regret and Shame

This scene touched me as a child, but it captivates me as an adult. We are all haunted by the thoughts and deeds of our past. Even believers recognize the power of abiding sin and the stinging sensation of remorse. We are in desperate need for our guilt to be removed from us as far as the East is from the West. But guilt never travels alone.

Guilt begets regret. Regret begets shame. And the three cling to us mercilessly. At first we embrace them out of a sense of obligation, only to discover that they are not our allies. They will suffocate and kill us if they can have their way.

This can be seen in a powerful way in Robert P. Tristram Coffin's poem "Forgive My Guilt," which recounts a childhood act that haunted him throughout adulthood. The poem describes a time when he fired a pellet gun at two birds for fun. His shots maimed the birds and left them flightless; their shrieks never to be forgotten.

Throughout his life he would hear their cries "over all the sounds of sorrow in war or peace / I ever have heard, time cannot drown them." He concludes with these gripping lines:

> But I have hoped for years all that is wild,
> Airy, and beautiful will forgive my guilt.[3]

The years did not diminish his sense of shame over this youthful act. Nature itself bore witness against his crimes and turned a blind eye and deaf ear to his lifelong pleas for mercy.

The poem powerfully illustrates that the weight of our guilt will eventually crush us. It is a disagreeable travel partner and an unhealthy bedmate. David exemplified this in the Psalms:

If you, O LORD, should mark iniquities,
    O Lord, who could stand?
But with you there is forgiveness,
    that you may be feared. (Ps. 130:3–4)

Our souls are in bondage to our guilt. We cannot stand beneath the burden of our iniquities. We will find freedom only in forgiveness. But if God does indeed exist, how can we as guilty humans ever merit his mercy?

The Colossians Quotient: Grace Is the Guilt Antidote

The Bible makes it clear that no one deserves grace. In fact, this is the very definition of grace, that it is unmerited kindness. God's goodness should lead us to repentance. Jesus who knew no shame, because he had no regrets, took upon himself all of our guilt. He took it out of the way and nailed it to his cross. In Christ we can be set free from guilt's cruel tyranny because Jesus offers to exchange our moral failure with his perfection. The apostle Paul describes it in this manner:

And you, who were dead in your trespasses and the uncircumcision of your flesh, God made alive together with him, having forgiven us all our trespasses, by canceling the record of debt that stood against us with its legal demands. This he set aside, nailing it to the cross. He disarmed the rulers and authorities and put them to open shame, by triumphing over them in him. (Col. 2:13–15)

This isn't a new theme for Paul. His favorite description for those who do not trust Christ as Savior and Lord is the word *dead*. In our guilt, regret, and shame, the word *dead* makes perfect sense. It resonates with our inner experience. We are in need of life, abundant life. Guilt is systematically killing us.

We are unlike zombies, who appear to be dead on the outside yet are still animated. Our inner death is well concealed beneath layers of superficial life. We feel the pains of death from deep within. To quote Marcellus in Shakespeare's *Hamlet*, "Something is rotten in the state of Denmark." And we have the uncomfortable suspicion that it might be us.

Dead is an evocative word. I remember the day when this word brought my world crumbling down. I was maybe five or six years old. My older brother and sister and I were sitting at the kitchen table. My parents explained that a car had hit our family pet, a mutt affectionately named Buffy. That was the last time I saw her, until early the next spring when the winter frost was slowly fading from the midwestern landscape.

I remember the day well. I was playing outside. The flowers were in full bloom. Spring had arrived. And I found Buffy. Because the Illinois ground was frozen by the time of her dreadful accident, my dad had hidden her beneath a load of lumber next to our garage. And, unfortunately, he had forgotten about her entirely.

Needless to say, I was horrified. That is, once my initial enthusiasm was eclipsed by the realization that my frozen dog wasn't going to budge. The only command she would obey now was "stay." I guess I could add "freeze" or "play dead" to the list, but I digress.

While the story of Buffy is a little humorous (and perhaps a bit creepy), death in general is not something we laugh about. We tend to avoid the topic at all costs. But death is the category Paul uses to depict the human condition apart from Christ. Due to our idolatry and rebellion, we are spiritually dead and stand condemned before the Creator. Because we are out of sorts with the moral code— the third impulse—a central part of our being is dead on the inside. And it plagues us with frequent reminders of our failures.

The human experience is tragically stained by guilt, shame, and regret. But these are only symptoms. Sin— our rebellion and idolatry—is the real culprit. It was on the cross that Jesus, as Paul says, became sin for us that we might become "the righteousness of God" in him

(2 Cor. 5:21). He traded his righteousness for our unrighteousness, so that in him we might find life. The gospel is God's cure for our spiritual death.

The problem is sin. The symptom is guilt. The solution is the gospel.

Modern medicine offers the hollow promise of removing our guilt as if doing so were as simple as treating symptoms of depression with drugs. While such medications have been helpful for many, we should see through any utopian vision of total healing. We intuitively know there is a deeper problem. The way to remove our guilt is not found in suppressing our feelings. Our guilt, in terms of our position of being guilty, must be *categorically* changed.

Deep down we know that we can't do this on our own. Our moral equilibrium is out of whack. *We* can't fix *us*. Someone with the appropriate authority must declare us "not guilty" and begin to change us from the inside out.

Sin is a cruel master, and her offspring—regret and shame—will torture us in our despair. We have no hope apart from total and absolute clemency. And this is exactly what the gospel offers us.

Notice Paul's use of the word "all" in the Colossians passage: God has "forgiven us *all* our trespasses" (Col. 2:13). What if Paul were not inspired to use the word "all"? On the one hand, if Jesus had forgiven us *some* of our sins, we should nonetheless be grateful. If your bank forgave *some* of your credit card bill, surely you wouldn't grumble. You wouldn't complain to a manager. In fact, you would probably send a thank-you note. Would you argue if *most* of your car loan were forgiven? Certainly not!

If Jesus forgave *most* of our sins, he would be gracious to do so. He would be worthy of all of our praise. This would be cause for great rejoicing.

On the other hand, we would still be enslaved to guilt, regret, and shame. And we would still face the wrath of God. Partial forgiveness wouldn't get us very far. We would still bear the weight of God's just judgment of our rebellion. Even if *most* of our sins were forgiven, a holy God would not tolerate sin's residue. We must be wholly clean, and therefore we must be wholly forgiven. We must be holy.

This is specifically the point of the gospel: Jesus has taken all of our sin. And faith in him cleanses us from all transgressions and all unrighteousness. Jesus bore the full weight of our sin in our place. As our substitute he took it *all*. He took it *all* out of our way. He nailed it *all* to his cross.

What if the burdens of our past mistakes really can be removed? Perhaps we are carrying them in vain. Maybe it's time to encounter grace. It's time to come to the cross.

Like Bunyan's pilgrim, you can be pardoned. At the cross you will find great mercy and discover that it is as abundant as it is free. This is clearly illustrated in the hymn "It Is Well," penned by H. G. Spafford:

My sin, oh, the bliss of this glorious thought!
My sin, not in part but the whole,

Is nailed to the cross, and I bear it no more,
Praise the Lord, praise the Lord, O my soul!

While guilt's ill-conceived children, regret and shame, may still taunt you, they will have no power over your future. They were nailed to a splintery post on Golgotha's hill. They are now dead. And, in Christ, you can now truly live.

Zach has heard this simple appeal many times. The story of the gospel is not new to him. His mind quickly recalls lengthy alter calls accompanied by multiple verses of the hymn "Just As I Am." This church scene is a bit humorous for him to consider now in the ominous shadows of brick towers and looming libraries. Yet there are those moments, for whatever reason, when he stops long enough to consider, What if it's really true?

The Gospel Offers Meaning for Our Mortality

Between us and Heaven or Hell there is only life,
which is the frailest thing in the world.

Pascal[1]

Some movies are so good even the popcorn tastes better. And there's nothing more relaxing than a two-hour respite in an air-conditioned theater with padded chairs and surround sound watching a sci-fi apocalypse. But whether it's Will Smith or Shia LaBeouf battling shiny anthropomorphic robots or all-seeing mega-computers, the sagas generally end the same way. Every plot about futuristic advances in artificial intelligence ends in either the demise of humanity or the destruction of machines.

The real-life discipline of artificial intelligence was actually created in 1956 when a small group of scientist meeting at Dartmouth College first coined the term. They gathered to investigate the possibilities of programming machines to simulate every form of human intelligence. While this emerging discipline offers many benefits, its limitations are unmistakable. I have no doubt that advances will continue to be made in this field, but could it be that there are some things about what it means to be human that will never be replicated?

Consider this: What if we are more than the sum of our parts? What if all the attempts at imitating human intelligence fail because we are actually more than machinery? The answers to such questions lead to even more pressing concerns, like: What if this life is only the beginning and death is not the end? What if some part of the human personality survives beyond the grave? What if we really do have a soul?

When you breathe your last breath, you will know. You will either know that God is real or know nothing at all. If there is no God, you will simply enter into what is romantically called eternal rest. This euphemistic terminology is a polite way to describe what it means to no longer exist. But if there is a spiritual part of your being that abides beyond the grave, then you will know full well the reality of the Creator.

Just Dust?

If the grave is the end, then there is no hope beyond death. Funerals are final. Our loved ones, now mourned, will never be seen again. There is no hope in death apart from the gospel. If we are nothing more than matter and machinery, then the old song by the band Kansas is right: we are dust in the wind, and no amount of money can buy us another minute once our time is up.

If we are nothing more than dirt, then there is no objective ground for hope. We will all ultimately die, and in the long run no one will remember our names. The human experience thus culminates in nothingness. If this is reality, we should all come to grips with our finite fate. The poem "Lament," by Edna St. Vincent Millay, captures the confusion over death that is inevitable if it is indeed the end:

Listen, children:
Your father is dead.
From his old coats
I'll make you little jackets;
I'll make you little trousers
From his old pants.
There'll be in his pockets
Things he used to put there,
Keys and pennies
Covered with tobacco;
Dan shall have the pennies
To save in his bank;
Anne shall have the keys
To make a pretty noise with.
Life must go on,
And the dead be forgotten;

> Life must go on,
> Though good men die;
> Anne, eat your breakfast;
> Dan, take your medicine;
> Life must go on;
> I forget just why.[2]

The widow in the poem is certain of her husband's death, but unsure why life must go on. The routine of daily life is unavoidable, but why must life itself persist? The perplexity illustrated in the poem seems inescapable if there is no afterlife.

But what if we really are more than organic parts and genetic processes? What if we are more than dust in the wind? What if life has an ultimate meaning? What if your life can be filled with a transcendent purpose?

A Hedonistic Fairy Tale

Let's look for answers in what can seem like the most depressing book in the entire Bible. Nearly every word in the book of Ecclesiastes drips with nothingness. I grew up hearing the story of how King Solomon was the wisest person to ever live. But after reading Ecclesiastes I had to question whether or not I had been lied to all my life.

The book summarizes Solomon's intellectual and hedonistic escapades that led him to conclude that life is meaningless. Without the final chapter, the book would end with little to no hope. But there Solomon encourages his readers to "remember also your Creator in the days of your youth," before death comes and "the dust returns to the earth as it was, and the spirit returns to God who gave it" (Eccles. 12:1, 17).

In this passage Solomon points to two foundations that frame reality: the existence of God and the immortality of the soul. Even the skeptical philosopher Immanuel Kant could not avoid these truths. Kant rejected the traditional arguments for the existence of God, yet he recognized that ideas like justice are meaningless without a perfect judge and if humans don't possess an immaterial, immortal soul. That's why theologian R. C. Sproul says Kant kicked God out of the front door and then smuggled him in the back door.[3]

Solomon concludes his book by underscoring the most important task of life, which is to be properly related to the Creator of the universe. What if Solomon is right? What if Kant was right? What if there is a God and we actually have a soul? Isn't acknowledging this the first step in finding purpose?

The Colossians Quotient:
A God Above, Therefore Meaning Below

We live every day as if there is more to life than matter. We value things like love, nobility, and beauty. We live as though our lives have some higher meaning beyond mere survival and the spreading of our genes. We live on what Christian apologists call "borrowed capital." Our optimistic outlook is actually due to interest drawn from a Christian view of reality (i.e., the gospel).

If there is a God above, then we can experience objective meaning below. Paul reminds the Colossians that their hope is not to be found in this world. He points them to the source of the joy:

> If then you have been raised with Christ, seek the things that are above, where Christ is, seated at the right hand of God. Set your minds on things that are above, not on things that are on earth. For you have died, and your life is hidden with Christ in God. When Christ who is your life appears, then you also will appear with him in glory. (Col. 3:1–4)

We are inclined to seek significance in our acquaintances, our assets, and our accomplishments. Give it enough time, accumulate enough stuff, exert enough influence, and we will fill the emptiness our hearts experience in the quiet moments when our thoughts become reflective. And yet our void remains unfilled.

In contrast, Paul tells the Colossian believers to seek joy and fulfillment from above. He tells them to set their eyes on things above. This does not mean Christians devalue the world below; they simply recognize that its intrinsic worth comes from outside itself.

In short, we have meaning below because there is a God above.

The opposite is also true: if there is no God above, we

cannot have objective meaning below. History is filled with influential thinkers who recognized this grim reality. Friedrich Nietzsche was one of them. Many consider him the father of nihilism.

Nietzsche knew that a godless world is ultimately a meaningless one. Many skeptics, however, do not take their worldview to this logical conclusion, and for good reason. History shows that nihilism is unlivable. Nietzsche is a perfect example of this. He once remarked, "The thought of suicide is a great consolation: by means of it one gets successfully through many a bad night."[4] No one wants to live in despair, so we all tend to embrace a sort of optimistic outlook. The real question is, then, is our optimism justified?

The playwright Samuel Beckett illustrated a nihilistic outlook in his play *Breath*. The roughly thirty-second presentation begins with a dark theater and the sound of a baby's cry. The stage is progressively illuminated to reveal a pile of disorganized trash. Another audible cry is then heard before the lights fade back to black. The final act of the short play is the sound of an exhaled breath. This is life without purpose. This is life without God.

Lawrence Krauss disagrees. He demonstrates far more optimism for a godless universe than Nietzsche does. In an op-ed piece for the *Los Angeles Times*, he writes, "Imagining living in a universe without purpose may prepare us to better face reality head on."[5] Many, however, find such a worldview debilitating.

Confessions of an Atheist

In the book *Good without God*, Greg Epstein, secular humanist chaplain at Harvard University, criticizes Richard Dawkins for having nothing of value to say to a student struggling with the nihilism that he considers the logical conclusions of his atheism. The student admits that he is contemplating suicide and asks Dawkins for advice.[6] Dawkins encourages the young man to write his experiences on the Dawkins website and seek help from the broader atheistic community.

I found the following conversation on Dawkins's blog shortly after I read Epstein's book. And I can't help but think the person in the book and the blog are one and the same. Here is an excerpt of his original post:

> In the past few months I've been having, from what I understand the term to mean, nihilistic thoughts when pondering what I call "The Big Questions" (usually after a toke or two). I know that Richard and others have said before that you give life your own meaning and that we create our own purpose in life, but aren't we just really bull——— ourselves? I mean in a few hundred years we will all be dead and no one will remember our names or actions (maybe Richard, but you get my point). After that, in millions of years the human race will be gone and what will all this have meant? What end goal are we striving towards? Is existence really the only reason to persist in life? I am just having trouble caring about what seem to be triv-

ial activities in my daily life now. Why should I care what laws my government is passing anymore than I care about what laws the Assyrians were subjected to? What does it matter? All these questions! I'm sorry to dump so much out in a single post, but as I was lying in bed coming to terms with the fact that my life (and the entire universe for that matter) pretty much exists without meaning, I had what I suppose was a panic attack. It was a terrifying experience. Anyone else experience this?[7]

One of the responses to the blog post demonstrates a bold confidence: "Consider the following: Through science, we maybe [*sic*] able to find a cure for aging. It may even happen within your lifetime if you don't get yourself killed trying to make the most of it. Who says we can't have eternal life without spirituality." Is this really the hope for humanity, to find a cure for dying—eternal life without spirituality?

Who are we kidding? Botox can't work forever. No matter how much you tuck and trim, eventually gravity and the grave will do their work and win in the end. There is no fountain of youth. Not even one that comes in a bottle or through a syringe.

The comment about eternal life without religion evoked a response from the author of the initial blog post: "Which is what I am having trouble coming to grips with. I'm just a chemical reaction that the physical laws of the universe are trying to continue. I'm meaningless." It appears unavoidable: in the absence of God there is a nothingness that the world cannot defeat. Perhaps science will find a cure, but I'm not going to hold my breath.

It is deep within the human experience to long for more than this world has to offer and to live as though that "more" might actually exist. As C. S. Lewis once said, "If I find in myself a desire which no experience in this world can satisfy, the most probable explanation is that I was made for another world."[8] Perhaps the vast majority of humanity is wrong, but our experiences seem to teach us that we were made for more than the world can give us.

As King Solomon observed, "He has made everything beautiful in its time. . . . He has put eternity into man's heart" (Eccles. 3:11). The cosmos is filled with purpose because there is a God above. Our hearts are intrinsically and acutely aware that there is more to us than chemical reactions and laws of physics. Our short lives find meaning in the Creator of the heavens and the earth. Though death awaits us all, it is not the end.

Jesus presents meaning and significance for our short lives on this little planet. But if the gospel is true, then he offers much more. The grave is not conclusive. Death is not supreme. Nothing will not prevail.

All Good People Go to Heaven?

Zach, however, considers the doctrine that offers hope to so many to be one of Christianity's most repugnant features. The reward of the righteous loses its luster when viewed in contrast to the eternal damnation of billions of unbelievers. Award-winning journalist Lisa Miller gives a comparable critique in her book *Heaven: Our Enduring Fascination with the Afterlife.* "What I don't wish for—" Miller writes, "and this is my line in the sand—is any certainty about who's in and who's out."[9]

I empathize with her concern. The thought of anyone facing eternal punishment is hard for me to stomach too. But what if there is an afterlife and what if Jesus really is the only way? And what if we can never be good enough on our own to get there?

As I mentioned in chapter 4, the point of the gospel is that there really are no wholly good people. I once emceed an event cosponsored by the campus ministry I served with and the Society for Secular Students. Both groups spent time planning the event, and both invited a speaker to share on behalf of their respective side of the issue. The topic for discussion was the perennial debate over morality and God.

The Christian apologist began his talk by saying, "It's obvious that you can be good without God." Why did I invite this guy? Did he just give away the farm? Actually, I agree with his statement, particularly in light of what he said next.

He explained that everyone can be good with a little *g* but not with a capital *G*. He illustrated this by saying that everyone in attendance, nearly three hundred students who were mostly skeptics, held to some system of morality. All their moral codes were similar in many ways, and nuanced in others. Yet, no one held to even his or her own moral code flawlessly. They were *good* but not *Good*. In order to be *Good* they needed someone to obtain moral perfection on their behalf—even if by their own standards—and impute that Goodness into their account.

This really is the message of the gospel. We've all fallen short. Yet God offers bad people redemption through faith in Christ. If morally deficient humans can ever stand before a perfect God, it would seem that a process of replacing our wrong with his right is necessary. This is precisely what Jesus accomplished in his death and resurrection.

The ubiquitous assumption that heaven is only for good people is powerful because it is actually true. It's simply a matter of how you define and obtain goodness. If we don't measure up to our own standards, how can we ever meet God's? Yet God offers to clothe us in the goodness of Christ. If the gospel is true, then the grave is not the end. And if the grave is not the end, then the central task of breathing human beings is to prepare for what happens next.

The Gospel Offers Answers for Our Adversaries

Men despise religion; they hate it and fear it is true.

Pascal[1]

Zach is in no way militant toward those of faith. Like many humanist authors today, he wants to keep a healthy distance between himself and the often-toxic reputation of some New Atheist authors whose speech regularly takes a hateful tone. Zach has seen the ugly side of religion, but there are also fragments of his childhood religious experiences that possess a beauty for which he is still appreciative.

Yet, his reasons for dismissing Christianity are lingering and powerful. He doesn't want to be like the charlatan deacon in his home church known for telling racial jokes in the lobby before worship only to later voice the prayer for the weekly offering. And there's not one fiber of his being that resonates with the anti-intellectual ethos he experienced in Christian high school.

But what if his rejection of Christianity really has more to do with his repulsion to specific Christians, and to a certain brand of Christianity, than it does with the person of Christ? What if he applied the same sort of skepticism to his new worldview?

This reminds me of a personal testimony I recently heard from a man named John.[2] John's trajectory away from God was evident in high school. It matured in college. And it blossomed in adulthood. His life spiraled out of control after he graduated from a university. He went from using to selling cocaine. His drug use, alcohol abuse, and womanizing left him completely empty. He came to hate himself and everyone around him. He desperately needed intervention.

One evening he rented a movie with the hope that the amusement would momentarily distract his anxious heart. His entertainment of choice reflected his spiritual state. The film *Religulous*, featuring Bill Maher, had an ironic effect on John. He began the documentary skeptical of God. By the time he reached the credits, he had become skeptical of skepticism.

The overt bias of the production prompted him to find a more balanced presentation of the Christian faith. The video presented the all-too-common cultural depiction of Christianity as irrational and delusional. Atheistic authors like Richard Dawkins and Sam Harris wield these points relentlessly. While examples of fanatical belief or practice are easily found, the reader must move beyond the extremes and rhetoric and consider the central claims of the Christian faith.

Is Christianity irrational and delusional? Or does it offer a reasonable and compelling explanation of the human experience? Does the gospel require a blind leap of faith, or is it based upon historical facts?

On Cutting Off the Branch One Sits On

Skeptical friends often share with me their refusal to consider miraculous or supernatural explanations of the universe. Like Zach, they want something they can sink their teeth into, something they can see and touch. I empathize with this sentiment. But is this line of thinking logically tenable?

I often hear statements like, "I'll only accept what I can prove scientifically." This is, of course, a philosophical statement. It cannot itself be proved scientifically. You cannot see this truth through a microscope or a telescope. Is it thus false based on its own logic? It is certainly begging the question.

A careful look at the publications of the New Atheist authors reveals a strong reliance upon philosophical assumptions. Should their inability to build their arguments from a purely scientific basis concern skeptics? I'm reminded again of the words of Blaise Pascal: "Few men speak humbly of humility, chastely of chastity, few doubtingly of skepticism."[3] To borrow an expression from Pastor

Tim Keller, it is often necessary to doubt one's doubts. To be a true skeptic, a person should doubt even his or her own skepticism.

However, such challenges are often met—as one might assume—with a dogmatic trust that science will eventually remove the anomalies that plague a materialistic worldview. Just because science cannot give a convincing explanation *now* for basic human experiences like beauty, love, altruism, and morality doesn't mean it will be unable to do so sometime in the *future*.

But does blind optimism in the scientific method provide the kind of satisfaction we need for life's big questions? The idea that science will answer all questions in the end hints at a religious creed all of its own. Atheist Alex Rosenberg approvingly calls this view "scientism." It is up to the reader, however, to consider if this purely material explanation of reality best resonates with real-life experience. On the other hand, how might the gospel provide a compelling depiction of the human narrative?

The Effects of Easter

Christianity hinges on a historical event: the resurrection of Christ. And as an event that took place in time and space, Christianity is falsifiable. If the dead body of Jesus were found in the tomb, the Roman officials would have been extremely motivated to make this known. And if there were not good historical support for the resurrection, it could easily be dismissed today. Many have sought to disprove the historicity of Christianity on such grounds. In fact, Christian bookstores are riddled with the biographical works of researchers who endeavored to disprove the resurrection but were instead convinced of its veracity.

The apostle Paul places the resurrection as the central doctrine upon which the faith would stand or fall: "And if Christ has not been raised, then our preaching is in vain and your faith is in vain" (1 Cor. 15:14). Paul encourages his reader to imagine what the world would look like if the resurrection had not happened. If the resurrection were false, Paul says, then Christians would be liars who are still lost in their sins. There would be no hope.

But Paul does not leave the reader in despair. He counters his hypothetical postulations with the bold declaration, "But in fact Christ has been raised from the dead" (1 Cor. 15:20). If the resurrection is indeed a fact, then Christ's claims are validated and consequently Christianity is authentically true. It is then the task of every responsible critic of Christianity to examine the historicity of the resurrection.

Modern readers may find the challenge to explore the truthfulness of the gospel laughable. They shouldn't. It is curious that most are willing to accept a multitude of personalities and events from antiquity that offer far less historical support than Jesus's resurrection. Thus, the claim that the Christian faith is irrational is unfounded apart from an honest treatment of the resurrection. As Pascal stated,

"Let them at least learn what the religion is which they oppose before they oppose it."[4]

The apostle Paul provides a helpful model for explaining the resurrection in his first letter to the Corinthian church, wherein he quotes an early creed thought by most scholars to have originated within a few years of the crucifixion:

> That Christ died for our sins in accordance with the Scriptures, that he was buried, that he was raised on the third day in accordance with the Scriptures, and that he appeared to Cephas, then to the twelve. Then he appeared to more than five hundred brothers at one time, most of whom are still alive, though some have fallen asleep. Then he appeared to James, then to all the apostles. (1 Cor. 15:3–7)

Shortly after the crucifixion believers developed this simple creed to summarize Jesus's death, burial, and resurrection as the fulfillment of prophecies contained in the Jewish Scriptures. Paul uses its account of eyewitness testimony to corroborate the gospel witness. Paul is in effect telling his immediate audience that they can go talk to the eyewitnesses themselves, "most of whom are still alive" (1 Cor. 15:6). If the creed were fabricated, and if the eyewitnesses had not existed, this passage would have been easily refuted, and its inclusion in Paul's letter to the Corinthian church would make little sense.

But if Jesus did truly rise from the dead, then one should expect the sort of account and eyewitness testimony found within the creed. And for many scholars, the historical bodily resurrection of Christ makes the best sense of the empty tomb, the formation and exponential growth of the Christian religion, and the martyrdom of the early disciples. The Christian faith is neither irrational nor delusional if it is grounded in historical evidence.

The resurrection, if true, changes everything. The Christian need not say, "Christ has risen and *nothing* else matters," but rather "Christ has risen and now *everything* matters." The risen Christ sparked a flame that quickly spread across Jerusalem, throughout Judea, across Samaria, and to the ends of the earth. Taking the true tale of the resurrected Christ to every tribe and tongue is at the heart of the church's identity.

The Colossians Quotient:
A Strategic, Winsome, and Compelling Witness

That's why Paul did not shy away from opportunities to offer the gospel as the answer to our deepest questions. He asked the church in Colossae to pray for open doors so he could declare the mystery of Christ (Col. 4:3). And he regularly spoke in public settings, like Mars Hill in Athens, known for rational dialogue. He was neither ashamed of the gospel nor intimidated to share it with influential intellectual leaders.

But he was deeply concerned with the manner in which the gospel was presented. He gave this simple pattern for the Colossian believers to follow: "Walk in wisdom toward outsiders, making the best use of the time. Let your speech always be gracious, seasoned with salt, so that you may know how you ought to answer each person" (Col. 4:5–6).

Paul urged them to make the best use of their time. His words "walk in wisdom" accentuate a sense of intentionality and urgency. He knew they were prone to waste their opportunities with "outsiders." But not only was it possible for them to underutilize their encounters; even worse, they could actually ruin their witness. Zach is living proof that Christians can unwittingly push people away from Christ. The damage is often irreparable.

This reminds me of the haunting words from one minister: "The single greatest cause for atheism in the world today is Christians who acknowledge Jesus with their lips and walk out the door and deny him by their lifestyles. This is what an unbelieving world simply finds unbelievable."[5] Even if "cause" is too strong a word here, the conduct of professing believers bears on the credibility of their witness. Francis Schaeffer made a similar observation when he said that our lives are our "final apologetic."

Paul placed as much emphasis on the spirit of believers' interactions with the world as he did on the content of their message. Their evangelism was not to be without grace. They were to use well-seasoned words. Paul's analogy of salt was not an indication that he wanted them to supplement the content of their message. They were simply to draw attention to the extravagant qualities of the gospel.

I've never sunk my teeth into a freshly grilled steak

only to marvel at the taste of the salt. I've never sent my regards to the chef for the skillful use of this most basic seasoning. Salt magnifies its subject. The Proverbs use a similar metaphor:

> The wise of heart is called discerning,
>   and sweetness of speech increases
>   persuasiveness. . . .
> The heart of the wise makes his speech judicious
>   and adds persuasiveness to his lips.
> Gracious words are like a honeycomb,
>   sweetness to the soul and health to the body.
>   (Prov. 16:21, 23–24)

Paul makes it clear that the gospel comes equipped with answers. And he wasn't fearful of questions. The gospel claims to explain the sum of the human experience and more. Thus, believers should expect questions, and a lot of them. Paul tells them to be prepared. The apostle Peter offers a similar encouragement: "Always [be] prepared to make a defense to anyone who asks you a reason for the hope that is in you; yet do it with gentleness and respect" (1 Pet. 3:15).

Paul instructed the Colossians to make wise and winsome appeals for lost men and women to be reconciled to God. To love them is to listen to them. To listen to them is to empathize with their questions. And to empathize with their questions is to relate the hope of the gospel to their struggles.

The gospel alone is the Christian's final answer to humanity's search for ultimate truth. It is the Christian's end game; of this believers need not be ashamed. Nor should Christians be surprised when it is demonstrated as the power of God unto salvation for anyone who believes.

That's what happened for John. A movie making fun of God actually contributed to his conversion. When God promised to work all things together for good (Rom. 8:28), it seems that blasphemous documentaries were a part of the package. John sought a more thorough explanation of the Christian faith, which led him to the online teaching ministry of Ravi Zacharias, who systematically deconstructed his doubts. John was confronted with the authentic gospel, and he embraced it gladly.

Sometimes the greatest adversaries are within and not without. Christianity provided John with answers to the questions that plagued him the most. Today he is an active church member in a faithful church in Washington DC. In his testimony we see both the explanatory and the saving power of God's redemptive story.

Yet such stories aren't convincing for Zach. And I don't necessarily think they should be. But I do think Zach should honestly consider whether his trajectory away from Christianity is based on the central claims of the gospel or on the all-too-often ridiculous nature of many who profess faith. These are two very different issues.

If the resurrection is true, then racist deacons and anti-intellectual Christian teachers don't negate its authority or power. They do, however, illustrate that we are unworthy and that we all have a long way to go. At the same time, no faith is more multicultural and has motivated more intellectual inquiry than the worldview whose story of creation, fall, and redemption through resurrection wrestles honestly with our failures—and the process of overcoming them.

The Never-Ending Story

If our condition were truly happy, we [would]
not need diversion from thinking of it in order
to make ourselves happy.

Pascal[1]

Things really haven't turned out the way he always thought
they would. No moral metamorphosis has taken place. He
doesn't wear all black—well, not all the time, at least. He
hasn't grown fangs. He's not addicted to drugs. Honestly,
he's found happiness in a godless cosmos. He can't complain. It seems Nothing has been pretty good to him.

On most days Zach feels as though he made the right decision. He dismisses the other days as wishful thinking. He
is generally convinced there is no God. And he's now comfortable with the prospects of a universe devoid of deity.

He likens it to the ugly breakup of an unhealthy relationship. It was painful, but it needed to happen. It reminds me of a comment I once read from a skeptic: "You

Christians seem to have a religion that makes you miserable. You are like a man with a headache. He does not want to get rid of his head, but it hurts him to keep it."[2] Zach gave up the headache of religion a long time ago. And now the future seems bright.

Zach's story isn't uncommon to the biblical narrative, surprisingly enough. The New Testament writers didn't cover up stories of apostasy. It appears that God wants Christians to be well aware of the appeal of Nothing. Even one of the apostle Paul's closest co-laborers chose Nothing over Jesus.

The Colossians Quotient: The Sunny Side of Nothing

Paul's letters are punctuated with personal references. He concludes his Colossian epistle with a series of greetings, including the following: "Luke the beloved physician greets you, as does Demas" (Col. 4:14). At work between the lines in this short verse was Nothing. And Demas, like Zach, was paying close attention to its every move.

Paul later describes Demas's choice in a letter penned shortly before Paul's execution: "Do your best to come to me soon. For Demas, in love with this present world, has deserted me and gone to Thessalonica. . . . Luke alone is with me" (2 Tim. 4:9–11). Demas was enamored with another depiction of reality. He was comfortable with Nothing. So, it only seems natural that he chose the City of Man over the City of God.

Christians are too quick to dismiss Demas, however. It's not like they don't understand the appeal of Nothing. I have felt it myself. It's ironic, but it seems that Nothing people and gospel people face a similar struggle. Nothing people fight the appeal of the gospel. That's why some atheists describe being mad at God for not existing. Similarly, Christians—like King Solomon—fight the pull of nihilism.

Demas not only felt it—he followed it. Demas was "in love with this present world." But what exactly does that mean? We know he left the apostle Paul. He seems to have left missionary work altogether. It's probable he also left the faith. But why? Unfortunately, that is something we cannot know for certain, though Bible commentators speculate. Paul simply says that he went away because he loved this world. But is loving the world really so bad?

Maybe Demas divested himself in humanist efforts, like Zach. Perhaps he was busy learning from the "original source" philosophers of the Greek first century. Who wouldn't love to do that? Well, I personally would, though I recognize that endless discussions with philosophical eclectics might not be everyone's cup of tea. For whatever reason, Demas found something he wanted more than Jesus.

It seemed that Demas was betting the world would offer a better payoff. But what if the world can't deliver on its promises? We've all heard stories of wealthy and famous people who are miserable. Many, like Ernest Hemingway, unfortunately deal with their troubles by ending their own lives. If they, having much more than we, could not find fulfillment, why do we assume that our plight will be any better if we were to find fortune and fame? As celebrity Jim Carrey recently said on Twitter, "I wish everyone could get rich and famous and everything they ever dreamed of so they can see that's not the answer."[3]

What if an atheistic universe, despite John Lennon's song "Imagine," is more like Aldous Huxley's novel *Brave New World*? Huxley, writing in the early 1930s, sought to describe where society was heading through the use of a literary genre known as *futurology*. What was his vision of the future? He foresaw a genetically engineered humanity in pursuit of passion. Unfortunately, his futuristic picture of humanity doesn't lead to a happier existence. It is no utopia. The book ends with the central character hanging himself after a night of wild orgies.

When Huxley first wrote this novel, he actually felt that his depiction was a plausible portrayal of the future. And when he published the follow-up book *Brave New World Revisited* nearly thirty years later, he still held his original vision and even felt that society was moving in this direction faster than he originally thought possible. I'm not sure *brave* is the best word to describe his prophecy. *Scary* might be more appropriate.

What if, to return to an illustration from the introduction, in finding out there is no "monster" in the closet, we learn that Nothing has a far more negative force than we ever imagined possible? It could be that a godless world will turn out to be less like Peter Pan's Neverland and more like William Golding's *Lord of the Flies*, the novel about a group of young boys, stuck on a remote island, who sought to govern themselves, only to discover the darker side of human nature.

It reminds me of the scene from Pixar's *Toy Story 3*, the second animated sequel about a band of toys that belong to a boy named Andy. In this film Andy is now grown and preparing for college. While packing up his room, his mom accidently puts his childhood toys in a pile to be taken to the trash. The toys narrowly escape a menacing trash truck and hide in a box labeled for donation to the Sunnyside Day Care.

Upon their arrival at the day care they meet Lotso, a pink, strawberry-scented teddy bear who is clearly the head toy in charge. Lotso warmly welcomes the group and gives them a tour of their new home. He promises them they will have plenty of kids to play with five days a week. At this point in the story, Sunnyside appears perfect in every way.

Lotso's orientation outlines the benefits of the day care: "We don't need owners at Sunnyside. We own ourselves. We're masters of our own fate. We control our own destinies." For a brief time all the toys marvel at their newly discovered paradise. But to their horror, they learn that Lotso is a spiteful dictator who takes advantage of weaker toys. Their dream destination quickly becomes a nightmare. And the rest of the movie is about their meticulously planned escape.

I can't help being reminded of another movie, *The Never Ending Story*. The plot is about a young boy named Bastian who ducks into an old bookstore to elude a sinister group of bullies. The grumpy storekeeper warns him to keep away from a mysterious leather book with the seal of two intertwined snakes. His curiosity gets the best of him, and as soon as the owner turns around, Bastian races out the door with book in hand, leaving behind a note that he'll return it when he's finished.

In the book he discovers Fantasia, a world facing imminent destruction by an evil force known as "The Nothing." The empress of Fantasia grows more and more ill as the Nothing destroys everything, leaving darkness and void in its wake. In desperation she sends a young boy Bastian's age named Atreyu on a mission to stop the Nothing.

As Bastian reads, he realizes that somehow he is inexplicably connected to the world of Fantasia and that his thoughts and feelings have an odd influence on this make-believe world. Throughout the book the Nothing claims more and more of Fantasia, until it is on the brink of destruction. As her world crumbles, the empress cries out to Bastian for help. He then discovers that he alone can restore Fantasia through his thoughts and rebuild the empire one wish at a time.

Like Fantasia, our world is subject to nothingness. Like the people of Fantasia, we are in need of divine intervention. We can find meaning only if God endows our world with purpose. If he doesn't intercede, the Nothing will erode the very foundations of what it means to be human.

The Dark Side of the Nothing

The pages of history are spattered with blood from the relentless campaign of the Nothing. This is nowhere more clearly seen than in the horrors of the twentieth century. Two authors, one British and one Russian, provide poignant summaries of these genocides while pointing to the gospel as the only power strong enough to stop the Nothing.

Dorothy Sayers, one of the first female graduates from Oxford University, delivered a prophetic speech titled "Creed or Chaos" in the spring of 1940. She warned her audience of the nature of Britain's imminent clash with Germany. She said the conflict would not be primarily due to politics or power, but instead "a violent and irreconcilable quarrel about the nature of God and the nature of man and the ultimate nature of the universe."[4]

Sayers sought to simplify the conflict by reducing the issues to two categorical options. Hitler had embraced isolated doctrines of Nietzsche's philosophy. His saw himself as the "superman" who would lead the people to a pure race. A rejection of the foundations of Christianity, she said, led to this seething turmoil. The alternatives, as she saw them, were Christianity (creed) or a form of nihilism (chaos). For Sayers it was plainly Jesus or Nothing.

Sayers recognized the power of the gospel to sustain

society. And she saw the imminent war as an opportunity for the church to reclaim its offer of the gospel as the fountainhead from which all blessings flow:

> This is the Church's opportunity, if she chooses to take it. So far as the people's readiness to listen goes, she has not been in so strong a position for at least two centuries. The rival philosophies of humanism, enlightened self-interest, and mechanical progress have broken down badly; the antagonism of science has proved to be far more apparent than real. . . . The thing that is in danger is the whole structure of society, and it is necessary to persuade thinking men and women of the vital and intimate connection between the structure of society and the theological doctrines of Christianity.[5]

Sayers's words were validated with bombs and blood. Shortly after her speech Hitler launched an intense campaign on England, concentrated on London, resulting in over forty thousand deaths from fifty-seven consecutive nights of bombing. But the British civilian fatalities paled in comparison to the millions of Holocaust victims. Sayers presented the gospel as the exclusive remedy to the chaos.

But Nietzsche's ideas were not limited to Nazi Germany; they permeated the ideologies of the Soviet Union as well. Bernice Rosenthal, professor of history at Fordham University, observes, "Nietzschian ideas infused Stalin's projects."[6] Like Hitler, his "will to power" resulted in mass bloodshed.

The Russian Noble laureate Aleksandr Solzhenitsyn summarized Stalin's horrific regime with these telling words in his 1983 Templeton Address:

> I have spent well-nigh fifty years working on the history of our Revolution; in the process I have read hundreds of books, collected hundreds of personal testimonies, and have already contributed eight volumes of my own toward the effort of clearing away the rubble left by that upheaval. But if I were asked today to formulate as concisely as possible the main cause of the ruinous Revolution that swallowed up some sixty million of our people, I could not put it more accurately than to repeat: Men have forgotten God; that's why all this has happened.[7]

At his address he made an appeal for Western leaders to take seriously their Christian foundations. He unashamedly pointed his audience to God as the sole remedy for societal decline, saying, "All attempts to find a way out of the plight of today's world are fruitless unless we redirect our consciousness, in repentance, to the Creator of all: without this, no exit will be illumined, and we shall seek it in vain."[8]

Like Sayers, Solzhenitsyn understood humanity's options within the categories of Christianity or inevitable chaos. He recognized that even the corruption of "an officially imposed atheism" and state communism were "doomed to never vanquish Christianity."[9] He acknowledged that Christianity alone could prevail against the encroaching secularism.

This is not to draw a direct line of causation from atheism to the horrors of Hitler's Germany or Stalin's Russia. Yet the shared value for Nietzsche's philosophy demonstrates that nihilism could not provide an objective basis for regulating evil practices. And Sayers and Solzhenitsyn believed that the horrors of history were prone to repeat themselves without the staying power of the cross.

Sadly, the Christian church is not without its own tragic shortfalls and scandals. Yet, the teaching of Christ provides clear parameters for human conduct. That's why to the extent that Christians do harmful things, they act unlike the Christ they (and we) profess to follow. They must violate their own beliefs in order to perform evil. Jesus, when taken seriously, provides an objective basis for human flourishing.

The gospel is the anti-Nothing.

The gospel gives an explanation for our existence, clarity for our confusion, grace for our guilt, meaning for our mortality, and answers for our adversaries. The gospel makes sense of the world while filling life with meaning and purpose.

Yet the Nothing baits its barbed hook with the trappings of this world. In its nets reside the captives of emptiness and despair. As C. S. Lewis once said, "Aim at Heaven and you will get earth 'thrown in': aim at earth and you will get neither."[10] History is ineradicably marked by humankind's choice between these two story lines: Jesus or Nothing.

I'm thankful Jesus once asked his disciples if they planned on leaving him like so many others had done. Peter's response is epic: "Lord, to whom shall we go? You have the words of eternal life" (John 6:68). Apart from Christ there are no objective explanations, no certainty, no grace, and no ultimate meaning. He alone possesses the words of eternal life. For the first-century disciples, and for us today, it is simply Jesus or Nothing.

Conclusion

The Weight of the Wager

> If you gain, you gain all; if you lose, you lose noth-
> ing. Wager, then, without hesitation, that He is.
>
> Pascal[1]

The choice seems easy. The world's offerings are plentiful. In contrast, Jesus offers a life of self-sacrifice and surrender. "Take up your cross daily," he says, "and follow me." At face value, the world has the obvious upper hand.

If atheism is true, then Christians really are a pathetic and delusional lot. They miss out on worldly pleasures in deference to something better. And if death is final, then all their hoping seems in vain. We must make our own destinies. We are the masters of our own fates. We are the captains of our souls.

Is it possible to create our own purpose and manufacture our own hope? Does the loss of God really have to ruin things on earth? Isn't it feasible to defy the doom and gloom and stare into this reality with bold optimism?

One contemporary author offered these words of encouragement: "If logic tells us that life is a meaningless accident . . . don't give up on life. Give up on logic."[2] But can we ignore the path that the logic of our worldview leads us down?

The Line of Despair

This process of coming to grips with the grim conclusions of our ultimate commitments is something Francis Schaeffer described as crossing "the line of despair." He believed that every worldview apart from the gospel must lead to some form of nihilism. Apart from a personal Creator, the cosmos doesn't offer objective hope. So if a person wants to climb above the line of despair apart from God, he or she has nothing objective upon which to stand.

This would be equally true for Christians if the gospel were false. The apostle Paul says as much when he asserts that if the resurrection is not a reality, then believers should live for the moment (1 Cor. 15:32–33). In this passage Paul quotes a common expression claimed by Epicurean philosophy: "Let us eat and drink, for tomorrow we die." Then he adds another saying from Greek culture when he quotes the poet Menander: "Bad company ruins good morals." This juxtaposition of quotations in the biblical text seems to illustrate two routes humanity takes in departing from God: hedonism or humanism.

Paul uses these same categories in the opening chapters of Romans. In rejecting God humankind will either live for pleasure or seek to establish some form of righteousness apart from God. If the cosmos is all there is or was or ever will be, then these are the only options. But can humanism or hedonism really satisfy our deepest needs? Can the world offer us fulfillment for what it means to be human?

The world is cold and uncaring, and there is nothing we can do to make it otherwise. We can't make the cosmos care. So our desire to be consistent with our ultimate beliefs forces us below the line of despair. Both hedonism and humanism end in despair. In the former, pleasures eventually fail us; and in the latter, we will fail ourselves. But if our worldview is unable to logically provide the satisfaction we seem to need, perhaps we can just defy logic.

We might, for example, heed the lyrics of the late eighties song, "Don't Worry. Be Happy." But this gleeful enthusiasm rings hollow in a world whose major anthem is written in a minor key. And it's difficult to turn off our brain and live with such a cheerful outlook if the facts don't support our case. If life begins and ends in nothingness, how can we act as though it has some sort of intrinsic significance in the middle? Can we live with a lie, knowing there is really no objective value to human life?

In the movie *The Words*, a struggling author discovers an unsigned manuscript and publishes it as his own. His wife and his agent believe he has found the creative inspiration to finally produce a masterpiece. Fame and fortune quickly follow. But he's haunted by the fact that all of the accolades have been gained through falsehood. His success is built on a lie.

In a similar way, how long can we maintain a hopeful perspective if it doesn't align with an honest view of reality? If our values flow from our fundamental commitments, then we have no alternative but to fall below the line of despair. The principles we esteem the most are not in harmony with our particular view of reality. Only the gospel can bring optimism and realism together by offering objective hope. As John's Gospel describes, it is in the incarnation that truth and grace are realized (John 1:17). In Christ, reality is aligned with optimism.

If there is a personal Creator who has visited us in our despair, then and only then can we rise above despair. As C. S. Lewis once wrote, "In the Christian story God descends to re-ascend. . . . He goes down to come up again and bring the whole ruined world up with Him."[3] In the gospel we are offered a worldview that allows us to consistently and logically live above the line of despair. And because, as Paul said, "in fact Christ has risen from the dead," our optimism is not in vain. It is sufficiently grounded in historical fact.

But what if we bet God doesn't exist? What if we live as though the gospel is false only to find that it is true after all? What if we, like Demas, make living for the world our highest priority?

Jesus actually spoke to this situation. "For what does it profit a man to gain the whole world," he once asked, "and forfeit his soul?" (Mark 8:36). If the world is not an end in itself, as atheism claims, then those who live only for this world will do so at the loss of something real, something eternal. They will gain the world at the expense of their soul.

But if the gospel is true, then the world's reward is only momentary, fleeting, and transitory in comparison to a future glory that will be revealed for those in Christ. And this is to say nothing of the Christian doctrine of hell, a doctrine clearly taught in Scripture. Jesus said that we should not fear the ones who could only kill the body, but should fear the One who could destroy both the body and the soul in hell (Matt. 10:28). Presupposing wrongly about God's existence is a costly matter.

And now we return to Pascal's wager. Pascal urged his readers to consider the radical implications of the gospel. The Nothing offers ephemeral pleasure. Jesus promises abundant life. Christians experience fulfillment in this life, but if Christianity is true, they will receive much more. Central to Pascal's writings is the understanding that the Christian merits *nothing* but gains *everything*:

> Now, what harm will befall you in taking this side? You will be faithful, honest, humble, grateful, generous, a sincere friend, truthful. . . . I will tell you that you will thereby gain in this life, and that, at each step you take on this road, you will see so great certainty of gain, so much nothingness in what you risk, that you will at last

recognize that you have wagered for something certain
and infinite, for which you have given nothing.[4]

Pascal realized the benefits of believing in Christ for
both this life and the next. He wasn't calling skeptics to
offer God a passing nod in order to better their odds. He
sought to illustrate the gospel's ability to answer humanity's existential needs for certainty and fulfillment, but
more importantly, the gospel's sufficiency to satisfy our
eternal need for salvation.

The gospel lifts humanity above the line of despair.

The Italian Renaissance artist Michelangelo illustrated
these truths in his famous paintings in the Sistine Chapel
in Rome. The ceiling of the chapel is covered with beautiful scenes from the Genesis narrative. The creation account
is contrasted with another mural by Michelangelo, on the
wall behind the altar, depicting the biblical scene of the
final judgment. The artwork portrays the reality of a Creator who is both Judge and Redeemer.

Like Michelangelo's art, the human experience points
us upward. The basic and intuitive instinct to attribute
intelligence to the formation and governance of the created world, and the inescapable feeling of guilt that we are
somehow out of sync with this cosmic power—these both
point to the gospel. They point to a Creator. They reveal
our need for a Redeemer.

But in our depravity we shun these truths. They are too
great for us. We seek diversions in amusements. We guard

our autonomy at all costs. We seek alternatives in plausible arguments and deceptive philosophies. But we cannot fill the void on our own. We cannot stop the Nothing. Our guilty and weary hearts betray this reality: we need the gospel to be true.

And the wonder of all wonders is that it actually is.

The human narrative finds its meaning in the events of Christmas and Easter. God has visited us in our despair. His incarnation shows us that he became like us. And his resurrection shows us that we will become like him. The gospel does not imply that Jesus has risen and *nothing* else matters, but rather that Jesus has risen and now *everything* matters. We can now live above the line of despair because the gospel is true.

Jesus the Redeemer stands with an iron foot upon the reptile throat of nothingness. The seizures of its body and its muffled moans still echo throughout the cosmos. But it is defeated. Don't believe its lies.

Michelangelo, in addition to his paintings, provided a poetic description of Christ's exclusive ability to stop the inescapable nihilism that invades a godless cosmos:

> Burdened with years and full of sinfulness,
> With evil custom grown inveterate,
> Both deaths I dread that close before me wait,
> Yet feed my heart on poisonous thoughts no less.
> No strength I find in mine own feebleness
> To change or life or love or use or fate,

> Unless Thy heavenly guidance come, though late,
> Which only helps and stays our nothingness.[5]

In the gospel we learn of Christ's heavenly guidance, which alone can suppress the nothingness threatening our existence. Our hearts will be restless, as Saint Augustine said, until they find their rest in him. Freedom can be found only in his divine intervention. And he has come. *And in the gospel he offers us everything.*

A Personal Decision

Throughout the book we have considered Zach's response to this dilemma. To be fair, Zach is really not one person, but a composite of personalities with whom I've shared meaningful dialogues about the gospel. I've even mixed a little bit of myself into his story.

It is my earnest prayer that "Zach" will reach the same conclusion as professor Mark Bauerlein (mentioned in the introduction). In his article "My Failed Atheism," he recounts his journey from atheism back toward Christianity:

> My atheism began with the perception of nothing, a meeting with the void, and it lay beyond refutation.
> . . . The process worked incrementally and backward, not toward faith but away from nihilism, fueled by the rising conviction that the conclusion I had drawn long ago was wrong. . . .
> After the authority of nihilism slipped, it was time to learn about the other side.[6]

Believers and unbelievers alike feel the draw of the gospel and the allure of the Nothing. In the end we will all have to make a decision between these two narratives. We must all draw a conclusion as to which story line accounts for the human experience.

The answers to these questions should be pursued at all costs and should never be taken carelessly. For the answers to these questions hold the key to understanding our past, our present, and our future.

Don't let the word *wager* fool you. This is no game. And you should not bet lightly. All of humanity stands at a cosmic crossroad facing the consequential choice between two stories: Jesus or Nothing.

Choose wisely.

Afterword

Marcus Gray (aka Flame)

I was obsessed with the world.
It offered me glitter not gold,
And I believed the lies it told.

Its promises were sweet;
It swayed my mind away from reality.

Its allure was strong;
It offered me life—but it was wrong.

Its emptiness drained my will to live;
I must be more than dust—just blowing in the wind.

It left me without purpose and hope—feeling somber.
Where did it get its strength—I wondered?

Why was I so in love?
I'm talking head over heels.
Why did I commit my way to Nothing
And its philosophical thrills?

But there was a historical figure they said was
     the Truth;
One who could free me from Nothing and its
     worldly noose.

They said His name is Jesus and that He is the way.
He offered me love, forgiveness, and grace.

I found true life in Him: said goodbye to the Nothing.
Eternal life I have gained: now end of discussion.

Acknowledgments

Since I've quoted Pascal so much along the way, it's only fitting that I include him here. He once said, "Certain authors, speaking of their works, say: 'My book,' 'My commentary,' 'My history.' . . . They would do better to say: 'Our book,' 'Our commentary,' 'Our history,' etc., because there is in them usually more of other people's than their own."[1] This could not be more true regarding this project! I need to thank a lot of people who helped make this book a reality. There surely is much here that is more than my own.

It's fitting, for innumerable reasons, that I thank Jesus first and foremost. I do believe that life really boils down to Jesus or Nothing. And I came to believe that not because of anything intrinsically good about me. I believe it because he, spiritually speaking, spit into clay, pressed it into my eyes, and gave me sight: I once was blind but now I see. That's why the only really good thing about me is Jesus.

April Joy, my amazing wife, is the one who came up with the idea of using *The Never Ending Story* as an illustration in the final chapter. It tied it all together nicely. Our twins, Isaiah and Micah, were born in the midst of my dissertation writing, and our first daughter, Addilynn Joy, was born during this my first book project. Poor Josiah, our thirdborn, is the odd man out. I'm so thankful for them all—most of all April, who continues to put up with me and all my projects.

Russell Moore, who penned the foreword to the book, is a dear mentor and friend. I'm convinced this book wouldn't have happened if it weren't for his initial encouragement. I'm his perennial theology student. I hope to never graduate from his influence. And I'll certainly never forget the Anne Lamott article he made me read after I finished my first draft.

Several people were kind enough to read various iterations of this manuscript: Zach Hensley, Sowmya Telaprolu, Andrew Walker; my mom, Nannette Braley; Ted Cabal, Timothy Paul Jones, Dan Dumas, and Mark McAllister. I appreciate their critiques, edits, and encouragement.

Marcus (Flame) and Crystal Gray are an amazing ministry tag team. I'm really looking forward to the album *Jesus or Nothing*, produced by Clear Sight Music. This is as close as I'll ever get to achieving my dream of becoming a rap star!

I'm indebted to the Southern Baptist Theological Seminary and Boyce College. They have provided me with many opportunities to teach on the topic of a Christian worldview. I'm certain that my ideas, however dull they might still be, are immensely sharper because of my time spent with the amazing leaders on our campus in Louisville, Kentucky.

Crossway took a gamble on me as a new author, and for that I must thank Dave DeWit. Though he spells his last name wrong, I still really appreciate all of his support and insight along the way. I'd also like to thank Thom Notaro for his invaluable help in the editing process. He is a wordsmith ninja.

And finally, I have to say a big word of thanks to everyone who was a part of the Campus Church during my time there. This book is the result of the three years we all spent together laboring for the gospel. It was a sweet season I will never forget.

Discussion Guide

This discussion guide is meant to help you get the most out of reading *Jesus or Nothing*. The following questions, arranged by chapter, are designed for use in a small group context. However, if you're reading this by yourself, this guide can also deepen your reflection on each chapter.

Introduction: The Power of Nothing

1. Does Zach's story sound familiar to you? Do you know anyone who has had similar life experiences?

2. Have you heard John Lennon's song *Imagine*? What do you think Lennon is hoping to convey in this song?

3. Summarize some of the differences the gospel makes for our worldview.

4. What do you think is meant by the phrase "human epic," at the end of the introduction?

5. Why do you think "Nothing" can be comforting at times?

Chapter 1: The Tale of Two Stories

1. What are the two worldview options from which every person must choose?

2. Recognizing that there are many religions and various ways of looking at reality, why do you think these two specific worldview categories are presented as the basic options available to humanity?

3. What does "Nothing" refer to in this book?

4. What are some of the specifics communicated about Jesus in this chapter?

5. What are two things the gospel shows us about humanity?

6. Summarize Pascal's "wager."

7. Why do you think Pascal's approach has been misunderstood and misused?

Chapter 2: The Gospel Offers an Explanation for Our Existence

1. What was your main takeaway from this chapter?

2. What is the main point of the Bible passage from the Colossians Quotient?

3. Why does this chapter say that the New Atheists have painted themselves into a corner with little or nothing to say about things that matter the most in life?

4. Why do you think the multiverse theory is popular among some atheistic authors?

5. What is the scope of the gospel's explanation of reality?

6. How does the gospel's account contrast with an atheistic explanation of reality?

7. What are some things you care about that cannot be studied scientifically?

Chapter 3: The Gospel Offers Clarity for Our Confusion

1. What was the main point of this chapter?

2. Why do you think the apostle Paul describes rival claims to the gospel as "plausible" or "persuasive"?

3. What are the different "layers of the onion" in the illustration about peeling back someone's worldview?

4. What is a presupposition?

5. What were the three points of critique, given in the *New York Times* book review, of Lawrence Krauss's claim that the universe came from nothing?

6. Why do you think the young lady in the opening of the chapter was struggling with the statement, "The gospel is true"?

7. Though Paul mentions the challenges of plausible arguments and deceptive philosophy, how does he describe the believer's faith, in Colossians 2:6–7?

Chapter 4: The Gospel Offers Grace for Our Guilt

1. What thought was the most memorable for you from this chapter?

2. What two things were described as "guilt's progeny"?

3. What is the root problem that leads to guilt?

4. What did C. S. Lewis mean by the "Moral Law"?

5. Describe the importance of Paul's use of the word "all" in Colossians 2:13.

6. Why do you think Paul favors the word "dead" for describing those who do not know Christ?

7. How does it make you feel to know that the person who has faith in Christ has been categorically changed from guilty to not guilty?

Chapter 5: The Gospel Offers Meaning for Our Mortality

1. What was the key point of this chapter?

2. Do you think scientists will ever be able to completely replicate the human personality through artificial intelligence? Why or why not?

3. According to the apostle Paul, where should the believer find his or her value?

4. Why do you think so many intellectual leaders, Christians and non-Christians alike, believe that atheism leads to some form of nihilism?

5. What did you think about the atheistic student's blog post about struggling with panic attacks when he thought about the logical conclusions of his worldview?

6. Why can there be no objective purpose here below if there is no God above?

7. Describe the difference between being good with a little *g* and being Good with a big *G*.

Chapter 6: The Gospel Offers Answers for Our Adversaries

1. What did you think of John's testimony from this chapter?

2. One author has suggested that people's belief in God, or lack thereof, is based on a mixture of three kinds of reasons: intellectual, emotional, and social. On which form of reason did this chapter focus most heavily?

3. What do you think the apostle Paul meant when he told the Colossians to "make the most" of their time with outsiders?

4. What is wrong with the statement, "I can only believe what I can prove scientifically"?

5. What do you think Francis Schaeffer meant when he said that the believer's lifestyle is the final apologetic?

6. How can believers season their words with salt when talking about the gospel?

Chapter 7: The Never-Ending Story

1. What does it means that Demas loved the world?

2. What does the Christian risk in living for another world if in the end this world is all there is?

3. What does the atheist risk in living for this world, if God really does exist?

4. How do Christians and atheists face a similar struggle when believers feel the pull of nihilism and atheists fight an inner desire for God to exist?

5. List some reasons why one might wish there were no God.

6. Both Christians and atheists can commit and have committed evil acts. Which worldview, when followed consistently, provides clear regulations for human conduct? Explain.

7. What is the "anti-Nothing"?

Conclusion: The Weight of the Wager

1. What was the main point of the conclusion?

2. What is the line of despair?

3. Mark Bauerlein is mentioned in both the introduction and the conclusion. In his article "My Failed Atheism," quoted in the conclusion, how does he describe his journey back toward faith in God?

4. The book concludes with the words "Choose wisely." Have you decided how you are going to respond to the gospel?

A Closing Prayer

The apostle Paul tells the young believers in Colossae of his struggle for them, which is a reference to his prayers that they would stand strong in the faith. It would be appropriate at the end this book, and this discussion guide, to make Paul's prayer our own: that our "hearts might be encouraged, being knit together in love, to reach all the riches of full assurance of understanding and the knowledge of God's mystery, which is Christ, in whom are hidden all the treasures of wisdom and knowledge" (Col. 2:2–3).

Notes

Introduction: The Power of Nothing

1. Mark Bauerlein, "My Failed Atheism," *First Things* (May 2012), accessed October 11, 2013, http://www.firstthings.com/article/2012/04/my-failed-atheism.

Chapter 1: The Tale of Two Stories

1. Arthur Bradley and Andrew Tate, *The New Atheist Novel: Fiction, Philosophy and Polemic after 9/11* (New York: Continuum, 2010), 10.
2. Ravi Zacharias, "Six Questions to Ask an Atheist," Ravi Zacharias International Ministries, accessed October 19, 2012, http://www.rzim.org/media/questions-answers/#.
3. Francis J. Beckwith and Gregory Koukl, *Relativism: Feet Firmly Planted in Mid-Air* (Grand Rapids: Baker, 1998), 69.
4. Ibid.
5. Alex Rosenberg, *The Atheist's Guide to Reality: Enjoying Life without Illusions* (New York: Norton, 2011), 18.
6. Ibid., 98.
7. Lawrence Krauss, "A Universe from Nothing" (lecture presented at the Atheist Alliance International Convention, Burbank, California, 2009); video available at http://www.openculture.com/2011/09/a_universe_from_nothing_by_lawrence_krauss.html.
8. Ravi Zacharias, *The Real Face of Atheism* (Grand Rapids: Baker, 2004), 153.
9. Ibid.
10. Alan Hájek, "Pascal's Wager," *The Stanford Encyclopedia of Philosophy*, ed. Edward N. Zalta, accessed June 2, 2012, http://plato.stanford.edu/archives/win2012/entries/pascal-wager/.

Chapter 2: The Gospel Offers an Explanation for Our Existence

1. Blaise Pascal, *Pensées*, trans. W. F. Trotter (Franklin, PA: The Franklin Library, 1979), 161.
2. Stephen William Hawking, *The Illustrated Brief History of Time*, 2nd ed. (New York: Bantam, 1996), 233.
3. Francis Schaeffer, *The Francis A. Schaeffer Trilogy: The Three Essential Books in One Volume* (Wheaton, IL: Crossway, 1990), 301.
4. Bertrand Russell, with introduction by Michael Ruse, *Religion and Science* (Oxford: Oxford University Press, 1997), 237.
5. Edgar Andrews, *Who Made God?* (Carlisle, PA: EP, 2009), 10.
6. Dorothy Sayers, *Creed or Chaos?* (New York: Harcourt, Brace, 1949), 28.
7. Fred Hoyle, "The Universe: Past and Present Reflections," *Annual Review of Astronomy and Astrophysics* 20 (September 1982): 16.
8. John Polkinghorne, *The Way the World Is: The Christian Perspective of a Scientist* (Louisville, KY: Westminster John Knox, 2007), ix.
9. The paper Antony Flew presented was "Theology and Falsification."
10. Paul Guyer, "Introduction: The Starry Heavens and the Moral Law," in *The Cambridge Companion to Kant and Modern Philosophy*, ed. Paul Guyer (Cambridge: Cambridge University Press, 2006); in Cambridge Companions Online, accessed January 22, 2013, http://universitypublishingonline.org/cambridge/companions/ebook.jsf?bid=CBO9781139001144.
11. Alex Rosenberg, *The Atheist's Guide to Reality: Enjoying Life without Illusions* (New York: Norton, 2011), ix.
12. C. S. Lewis, *Mere Christianity* (London: Geoffrey Bles, 1952), 31–32.
13. Ibid., 31.
14. Ibid.
15. Pascal, *Pensées*, 113–14.

Chapter 3: The Gospel Offers Clarity for Our Confusion

1. Blaise Pascal, *Pensées*, trans. W. F. Trotter (Franklin, PA: The Franklin Library, 1979), 124.
2. Lawrence Krauss, *A Universe from Nothing* (New York: Free Press, 2012), xiii.
3. From a debate between William Lane Craig and Lawrence Krauss,

North Carolina State University, March 30, 2011; transcript available at http://www.reasonablefaith.org/the-craig-krauss-debate-at-north -carolina-state-university.

4. Lawrence Krauss, "A Universe from Nothing" (lecture presented at the Atheist Alliance International Convention, Burbank, California, 2009); video available at http://www.openculture.com/2011/09 /a_universe_from_nothing_by_lawrence_krauss.html.

5. Krauss, *A Universe from Nothing*, 177.

6. Ibid.

7. David Albert, "On the Origin of Everything," review of *A Universe from Nothing*, by Lawrence Krauss, *New York Times*, March 23, 2012, Sunday Book Review, http://www.nytimes.com/2012/03/25/books /review/a-universe-from-nothing-by-lawrence-m-krauss.html.

8. Daniel C. Dennett, *Darwin's Dangerous Idea: Evolution and the Meanings of Life* (New York: Simon & Schuster, 1995), 21.

9. Albert Einstein, "Physics and Reality," *Journal of the Franklin Institute* 221 (1936): 349.

10. Nathan Frankowski, *Expelled: No Intelligence Allowed* (Premise Media Corporation, 2008), DVD.

11. Richard C. Lewontin, "Billions and Billions of Demons," review of *The Demon-Haunted World: Science as a Candle in the Dark*, by Carl Sagan, *New York Times*, January 9, 1997, Sunday Book Review, http://www .drjbloom.com/Public%20files/Lewontin_Review.htm.

12. Two good resources for considering this claim are James Hannam, *The Genesis of Science: How the Christian Middle Ages Launched the Scientific Revolution* (Washington, DC: Regnery, 2011), and Nancy R. Pearcey and Charles B. Thaxton, *The Soul of Science: Christian Faith and Natural Philosophy* (Wheaton, IL: Crossway, 1994).

13. Charles Darwin to William Graham, July 3, 1881, Darwin's Correspondence Project, accessed April 5, 2013, http://www.darwinproject.ac .uk/letter/entry-13230.

14. Thomas Nagel, *The Last Word* (New York: Oxford University Press, 1997), 130.

15. Nancy R. Pearcey, *Total Truth: Liberating Christianity from Its Cultural Captivity* (Wheaton, IL: Crossway, 2005), 34.

Chapter 4: The Gospel Offers Grace for Our Guilt

1. Blaise Pascal, *Pensées*, trans. W. F. Trotter (Franklin, PA: The Franklin Library, 1979), 50–51.
2. C. S. Lewis, *Mere Christianity* (London: Geoffrey Bles, 1952), 8.
3. Robert P. Tristram Coffin, "Forgive My Guilt," in *Apples by Ocean* (New York: Macmillan, 1950), 3.

Chapter 5: The Gospel Offers Meaning for Our Mortality

1. Blaise Pascal, *Pensées*, trans. W. F. Trotter (Franklin, PA: The Franklin Library, 1979), 64.
2. Edna St. Vincent Millay, "Lament," *Second April*, 4th ed. (New York: J. J. Little and Ives, 1924), 64–65.
3. R. C. Sproul, *The Consequences of Ideas: Understanding the Concepts That Shaped Our World* (Wheaton, IL: Crossway, 2000), 130.
4. Friedrich Nietzsche, *Beyond Good and Evil: Prelude to a Philosophy of the Future*, trans. Helen Zimmern (New York: Macmillan, 1907), 98 (aph. 157).
5. Lawrence Krauss, "A Universe without Purpose," *Los Angeles Times*, April 1, 2012, accessed April 2, 2013, http://articles.latimes.com/2012/apr/01/opinion/la-oe-krauss-cosmology-design-universe-20120401.
6. Greg Epstein, *Good without God: What a Billion Nonreligious People Do Believe* (New York: HarperCollins, 2005), 64.
7. I originally copied this from RichardDawkins.com, but it has since been removed from the website.
8. C. S. Lewis, *Christian Behavior: A Further Series of Broadcast Talks* (New York: Macmillan, 1946), 57–58.
9. Lisa Miller, *Heaven: Our Enduring Fascination with the Afterlife* (New York: HarperCollins, 2010), 247.

Chapter 6: The Gospel Offers Answers for Our Adversaries

1. Blaise Pascal, *Pensées*, trans. W. F. Trotter (Franklin, PA: The Franklin Library, 1979), 54.
2. John Joseph, "No Soul Is Too Far Gone to Reach," Together for the Gospel; video available at http://t4g.org/media/2012/09/testimonies-john-joseph/.
3. Pascal, *Pensées*, 104.
4. Ibid., 149.

5. This quote has been used by the contemporary Christian bands DC Talk ("What If I Stumble?") and War of Ages ("Intro") as a song introduction. It is widely attributed to Brennan Manning, though I cannot locate it in print.

Chapter 7: The Never-Ending Story

1. Blaise Pascal, *Pensées*, trans. W. F. Trotter (Franklin, PA: The Franklin Library, 1979), 165.
2. Quoted in Philip G. Samaan, *Christ's Way to Spiritual Growth* (Hagerstown, MD: Review and Herald, 1995), 133.
3. Jim Carrey, comment on Olivia Rosewood, "Please Meditate: Gratitude of Billionaires," *HuffPost Healthy Living*, November 28, 2011, http://www.huffingtonpost.com/olivia-rosewood/gratitude-and-wealth_b_1099954.html.
4. Dorothy Sayers, *Creed or Chaos?* (New York, NY: Harcourt, Brace, 1949), 29.
5. Ibid.
6. Bernice Rosenthal, *New Myth, New World: From Nietzsche to Stalinism* (University Park, PA: The Pennsylvania State University, 2002), 235.
7. Quoted in John H. Timmerman and Donald R. Hettinga, *In the World: Reading and Writing as a Christian*, 2nd ed. (Grand Rapids: Baker, 2004), 127.
8. Ibid., 151.
9. Ibid., 149.
10. C. S. Lewis, *Christian Behavior: A Further Series of Broadcast Talks* (New York: Macmillan, 1946), 55.

Conclusion: The Weight of the Wager

1. Blaise Pascal, *Pensées*, trans. W. F. Trotter (Franklin, PA: The Franklin Library, 1979), 68.
2. Harold S. Kushner, *When All You've Ever Wanted Isn't Enough* (New York: Fireside, 2002), 141.
3. C. S. Lewis, quoted in Will Vaus, *Mere Theology: A Guide to the Thought of C. S. Lewis* (Downers Grove, IL: InterVarsity, 2004), 82.
4. Pascal, *Pensées*, 70–71.
5. Michelangelo di Lodovico Buonarroti Simoni, "A Prayer for Strength,"

accessed January 10, 2013, http://www.public-domain-poetry.com /michelangelo-di-lodovico-buonarroti-simoni/a-prayer-for-strength -26181.

6. Mark Bauerlein, "My Failed Atheism," *First Things* (May 2012), accessed October 11, 2013, http://www.firstthings.com/article/2012/04 /my-failed-atheism.

Acknowledgments

1. Blaise Pascal, *Pensées*, trans. W. F. Trotter (Franklin, PA: The Franklin Library, 1979), 13.